I0519784

THE WAR
OF TIDES

Mustafa Nejem

PROLOGUE

The War of Tides is a captivating fantasy novel that unfolds in a futuristic realm dominated by powerful corporations overseeing vast oceanic territories. During a ruthless conflict to secure control over valuable marine energy sources, the young protagonist, Tristan, finds himself unwittingly drawn into the heart of this tumultuous struggle. In a world characterised by the pursuit of wealth, authority, and deceit, Tristan must skilfully navigate treacherous waters while grappling with perplexing decisions and uncertainty about whom he can trust.

CONTENTS

Chapter 1
THE SUBMERGED WORLD

Tristan, a young aquatic technician, was diving into the ocean. The sun barely filtered through the water's surface, sending light rays into the depths. As he descended rapidly, his dim LED lights illuminated the path, providing visibility in the dark. The underwater world was alive with the chorus of bubbles and songs of sea creatures, filling his ears as he plunged deeper and deeper into the blue.

Tristan's love for the ocean began in childhood when he spent countless hours exploring the vast blue waters. He was always fascinated by the diverse marine life and the uncharted depths of the ocean. As he grew, his passion for the ocean only intensified, and he decided to pursue a career as an aquatic technician. In his profession, Tristan was responsible for delving into the secrets of the deep sea and ensuring the proper functioning of underwater structures that sustained life underwater.

He would spend long hours underwater, examining marine life, studying the currents, and analysing the underwater environment. His dedication and love for the ocean were evident in his work, and he was always eager to learn more about the ocean's mysteries and share his knowledge with others.

Tristan descended further and reached a coral reef, where sea creatures danced around vibrant colours under the light of his suit. He swam carefully, observing the beauty of the world around him.

Tristan stood still as a curious moray eel emerged behind a rock, extending its undulating body towards him. The eel inspected Tristan's diving suit, reminding him of the astonishing diversity of the ocean. With a smile under his diving mask, Tristan continued to explore.

Tristan continued his descent into the reef, and suddenly, a massive shadow loomed over him. When he looked up, he saw a majestic manta ray. Its grandeur and exquisite beauty left him breathless. As he stretched out his hand towards the manta ray, he was reminded of the incredible connection he shared with the marine world by the gentle touch of its rough skin.

Tristan was not alone during his underwater exploration; his younger brother, Liam, accompanied him.

Liam, a novice diver, eagerly swam to his older brother Tristan and excitedly pointed at a manta ray, his eyes shining underwater.

"This is incredible, Tris! May I touch it?" Liam asked with excitement.

Tristan motioned for Liam to be careful as he stretched out his hand and touched the manta ray. Liam's face lit up with amazement as he felt the majestic creature's texture.

The two brothers grew up near the vast ocean, on the outskirts of the magnificent underwater metropolis of Aqualis. Their family had a strong passion for underwater exploration, a treasured tradition passed down through generations.

Their mother, a highly knowledgeable marine biologist, and their father, a dedicated employee of the Deep Tides of Neptec, the leading marine energy extraction corporation, had instilled a profound respect for the ocean and its enigmatic wonders from an early age.

Tristan and Liam admired the majestic manta rays when Tristan pointed towards a dark, mysterious abyss extending beyond the coral reef. Although Tristan was eager to explore the abyss, Liam was aware of the potential danger due to the strong underwater currents. Liam agreed to the adventure, and the two brothers set off towards the abyss.

As they dove deeper into the abyss, the water pressure increased, and the temperature dropped. The darkness enveloped their surroundings, but the lights on their diving suits were a constant guide. Despite the eerie environment, they were not scared; they were seasoned divers accustomed to these depths.

Tristan and Liam were fascinated when a bioluminescent creature swam past them, illuminating the water with its beautiful glow. They followed the creature without hesitation, feeling like explorers in a dream world as they observed the unknown marine life around them. They were amazed and thrilled by the breathtaking beauty of the underwater world.

The dive lasted for hours until Liam signalled their ascent. Tristan agreed, and the brothers returned to the surface, taking one last glimpse of the abyss before entering the sunlight.

Tristan and his brother emerged from the water, their faces filled with excitement and amazement. Tristan's mother, Emily, awaited them in a small boat.

"How was the dive, guys?" She asked with a smile. Tristan and Liam enthusiastically shared their experiences exploring the ocean and encountering various sea creatures, including a manta ray, bioluminescent creatures, and a mysterious abyss. Emily, who shared their love of the ocean, listened intently.

As Tristan and his family headed back to the coast of Aqualis, he couldn't help but think about the wonderful time they had spent together exploring the ocean. However, he couldn't shake off the troubling rumours he had heard about the escalating tensions between the corporations controlling the Deep Tides.

Although he preferred to stay away from politics and the greed of the business world, he suspected that he would soon be dragged into a much deeper conflict than he had ever imagined.

The ocean's beauty concealed dark secrets in its depths, about to be revealed to Tristan as his submerged world changed forever.

Tristan had spent his entire life in the submerged world, surrounded by the breathtaking beauty of the ocean. However, he was about to experience a life-changing event that would irreversibly alter the world he knew.

As he delved deeper into the ocean's depths, he realised that the beauty he had always admired was not without its dark secrets.

He would soon discover that the ocean was a place of both wonder and danger and that his perception of this mysterious world was about to be challenged like never before.

Chapter **2**

NEPTEC AND AQUADYNE

Tristan, Liam, and their mother, Emily, were in a small submersible, heading towards one of the massive underwater structures known as "Deep Tides." As they drew closer, the facility's sheer size and scale became more impressive. The afternoon sun filtered through the towering structures of steel and glass, which rose high above the ocean's surface, resembling giants of the sea.

Emily took the time to emphasise to her children just how crucial these facilities were. "The Deep Tides are the heartbeat of our underwater society," she explained. They power our underwater cities and fleets of watercraft and even provide electricity to coastal cities on the surface. Without them, our world beneath the waves would come to a standstill."

The submersible stopped before a colossal steel structure adorned with sparkling lights.

The towering structure was adorned with a luminous sign that read "Neptec", one of the two major corporations that held a tight grip on Deep Tides. As the name suggested, Neptec was a powerful underwater entity known for its cutting-edge technology and superior resources. The sign glowed brightly, casting a mesmerising aura that could be seen from afar, a true testament to the company's dominance and influence over the vast oceanic landscape.

Tristan stood there, gazing at the towering facility looming above him. The enormity of the Neptec building was overwhelming, and Tristan couldn't help but feel a sense of awe as he thought about the company's track record of pioneering breakthroughs in marine.

energy extraction. Neptec's impact on the subsea political and economic landscape was well-known and highly regarded. For Tristan's family, the corporation was more than just a name - it was a source of stability and security, as his father was employed at Neptec's Deep Tides division.

The company's success was deeply intertwined with their lives, and Tristan knew that the work within those walls would significantly impact their future.

Sin embargo, Neptec no estaba sola en el control de las Mareas Profundas. Otra corporación igualmente poderosa, Aquadyne, competía por la supremacía en la extracción de energía marina.

Emily pointed towards Aquadyne, another massive structure on the ocean floor, as they moved away from Neptec's Deep Tide in the submersible.

Aquadyne was a renowned company known for its unwavering commitment to advancing scientific research and developing state-of-the-art marine technology. Over the years, the company had established itself as a leader in the field, consistently pushing the boundaries of what was possible in underwater exploration. However, in recent times, the relationship between Aquadyne and Neptec has become increasingly strained due to their fierce competition for control over the Deep Tides.

The Deep Tides were the primary source of marine energy that sustained life underwater, and both companies were vying for dominance over this vital resource. As tensions continued to mount, the future of underwater energy production remained uncertain.

As Tristan and Liam drew closer to Aquadyne's Deep Tide, they couldn't help but notice the stark contrast between this facility and Neptec's. Aquadyne's facility was surrounded by a vast network of cutting-edge laboratories and research platforms, each one a testament to the corporation's unwavering commitment to advancing the frontiers of science and technology. The sheer scale and complexity of the facility left Tristan and Liam awestruck as they marvelled at the potential of what was being developed behind those sleek, futuristic walls.

As they continued their journey through Aquadyne's Deep Tides, Tristan thought about the enormous rivalry between the two corporations. Clashes and

legal disputes were common, and the struggle to control underwater facilities was a ruthless competition.

Neptec and Aquadyne were fully committed to gaining an advantage in marine energy extraction, widely considered the world's most valuable resource. Both companies were willing to go to great lengths to achieve their goals, including investing heavily in research and development, exploring new technologies, and forging strategic partnerships with leading industry players. Through their relentless pursuit of excellence, Neptec and Aquadyne aimed to establish themselves as the foremost players in the marine energy sector, with a clear edge over their competitors.

8

As the afternoon wore on, Emily ushered her two young children back to their home in Aqualis, the underwater megalopolis where they lived. During the return trip, she took the opportunity to explain to them the existence of a third player in the underwater corporate scenario: an underground network of rebels and ocean pirates vehemently opposed to Neptec and Aquadyne's growing influence.

These groups operated in the shadows, challenging the power and influence of the corporations and fighting for the cause of freedom and equality in the underwater world. Tristan and Liam listened to their mother's explanation with attention, their eyes widening as they took in the details of the rebels' activities. Despite their extreme methods, many in the underwater world sympathised with their cause, seeing in them the hope of change in a world dominated by corporate greed. Emily's detailed description of the rebels' activities painted a vivid picture of a world constantly in flux, with different factions vying for power and control. It was a world full of intrigue, danger, hope, and possibility.

As Tristan and Liam journeyed back to Aqualis, they deeply discussed their observations and insights gleaned from the day's events.

As Tristan and Liam journeyed back to Aqualis, they deeply discussed their observations and insights gleaned from the day's events.

It became increasingly evident that the struggle for control over the Deep Tides was not only a matter of economic dominance but also intricately linked to the political landscape, technological advancements, and power struggles within the underwater world. The bitter rivalry between Neptec and Aquadyne was not just a superficial clash but a complex web of animosity fraught with tensions that only continued to intensify. The future of the underwater world hung in the balance as the two powerful corporations vied for supremacy and dominance in this tumultuous and ever-changing landscape.

The moonless night stretched on, and Tristan stood transfixed, his gaze fixed on the distant horizon. The lights of the Deep Tides glimmered and danced on the inky black waters, an ominous sign of the gathering storm that would soon shatter his peaceful existence on the outskirts of Aqualis.

He knew that the underwater world was on the verge of a massive upheaval, a titanic conflict that would shake the very foundations of his world. And he found himself at the heart of the maelstrom, a lone figure caught amid forces beyond his control, struggling to survive and protect those he loved from the impending chaos.

Chapter 3

THE EXPLOSION

In the underwater megalopolis of Aqualis, Tristan was enjoying a peaceful night at home with his brother Liam. As they reviewed their notes from their last dive, their mother, Emily, a busy marine biologist, was on a work call. The underwater structures surrounding them were softly illuminated, casting a serene glow throughout their home. The sea life continued, and everything seemed to be in perfect harmony.

Suddenly, a deafening explosion shattered the peaceful atmosphere and shook the walls of their home. The sound echoed through the underwater city, leaving Tristan and Liam terrified and disoriented.

The brothers sprang into action in seconds and headed straight for the nearby port. The explosion had caused a massive shock wave that stirred up the waters around Aqualis, sending boats tumbling and damaging buildings.

As they arrived at the port, they were met with a chaotic scene of overturned vessels, damaged infrastructure, and frightened residents frantically gathering in the streets, trying to make sense of the situation.

Liam asked with a fearful expression, "What's going on?"

Tristan looked around in confusion, searching for answers. He approached a group of people, talking loudly, trying to understand the situation. He overheard bits of conversation about an explosion that had occurred at one of the Deep Tides, but no one had much information.

As he tried to gather more details, fear began to grip him. His mind filled with thoughts of his

mother, Emily, who worked at one of Neptec's underwater facilities and whether she was safe. With his heart pounding, Tristan took Liam by the hand and headed towards the nearest Deep Tide.

As our vessel approached the Neptec facility, the true extent of the destruction caused by the explosion gradually became clearer. The entire structure was contorted and shattered, with debris scattered everywhere. Intense emergency lights flashed incessantly from deep within the ocean, casting an eerie glow across the otherwise dark water. Despite the chaos, Neptec's emergency response teams worked tirelessly to manage the damage and locate

any workers trapped in the wreckage. The scene was one of utter devastation, and it was clear that this incident would have far-reaching consequences.

Tristan's heart pounded in his chest as he approached the chaotic scene of destruction. Smoke and debris filled the air, and screams and sirens filled his ears. He desperately searched for any sign of his mother, Emily, who worked in the Deep Tide area. His mind raced with worry and fear.

As he stumbled towards a group of emergency workers, his throat tightened with anxiety.

With his legs shaking and his voice quivering with emotion, he approached the workers and asked, "Excuse me, my mother works here. Can you please tell me if she's okay? Is she safe?"

The workers exchanged a worried glance before one stepped forward and reassured him, "We're doing everything we can to locate and assist everyone in the area. We'll do our best to find your mother and ensure her safety. In the meantime, please stand back and let us do our job."

Tristan nodded, feeling a glimmer of hope and relief. He stepped back, watching with bated breath as the workers continued their frantic efforts to rescue those in need. One of the workers noticed him and asked for his mother's name. After checking a list, the worker informed Tristan that Emily had been taken to an emergency medical centre on the surface due to minor injuries.

Tristan's heart was pounding with fear and anxiety when he heard the news of his mother's safety, but the thought of her being in danger had sent shivers down his spine. He knew he had to act fast. Without wasting time, he and Liam quickly boarded a rescue submersible that would take them to the surface. During the trip, Tristan couldn't help but think about what could have caused the explosion in Neptec's Deep Tide. Was it an accident or an act of sabotage? He had heard rumours about the rivalry between Neptec and Aquadyne and the growing tensions between the two corporations. He couldn't shake off the feeling that something wasn't right.

As the submersible emerged on the surface, Tristan and Liam rushed to the emergency medical centre where Emily was being treated. Tristan's heart sank as he saw his mother lying on the bed with a bandage on her arm.

He held his breath, praying that she was safe. Emily's face lit up with a tired smile as she saw them approaching her. "I'm okay," she told them, but the exhaustion in her voice was evident. "I was lucky. But this explosion... it's a real mess." Tristan and Liam hugged her tightly, relieved she was alive and unharmed.

Tristan rushed to inform his mother, Emily, about the explosion that had just occurred. He mentioned his suspicion that it might have been an act of sabotage, which made Emily visibly worried. I, too, was surprised to hear such a theory, which made me realise the gravity of the situation.

As the night progressed, news of the explosion at the heart of Aqualis, the bustling metropolis, quickly spread like wildfire, leading to widespread panic and fear among the residents. Realising the gravity of the situation, local authorities and corporations immediately launched investigations into the cause of the explosion. Still, the lack of information made it difficult to determine what had truly happened.

As the night progressed, news of the explosion at the heart of Aqualis, the bustling metropolis, quickly spread like wildfire, leading to widespread panic and fear among the residents. Realising the gravity of the situation, local authorities and corporations immediately launched investigations into the cause of the explosion. However, the lack of information made it difficult to determine what had truly happened.

The blast caused significant damage to the city's infrastructure, including the roads, buildings,

and transportation systems, disrupting the daily lives of the citizens. In the wake of the catastrophe, the people were left to deal with the explosion's aftermath while grappling with the uncertainty surrounding the incident. The explosion might have resulted from deliberate sabotage due to existing corporate tensions. However, the authorities remained tight-lipped about any leads or possible suspects, leaving the citizens to speculate and develop their theories. The uncertainty surrounding the incident only heightened the fear and anxiety that had gripped the people of Aqualis, leaving them wondering if they were safe in their city.

Tristan and his family arrived home exhausted and emotionally drained. As they lay down to rest, Tristan realised that his life had been forever transformed. The explosion at the Deep Tide had been a grim reminder of how fragile their underwater world was and of the powerful forces that move beneath the ocean's surface.

Some unforeseen events suddenly disrupted the peaceful and serene life they had enjoyed so far, and they were about to embark on a journey that would test their limits and push them to new heights. The road ahead was full of twists and turns they could

never have imagined, but they were determined to face the challenges head-on and emerge victorious. The transformation that awaited them was profound and would change their lives in ways they could never have anticipated.

Chapter **4**

THE SEARCH FOR ANSWERS

Tristan had spent a restless night, plagued by nightmares about the explosion at Neptec's Deep Tide. In the morning, light filtered through the windows of his house, but his mind was still full of unanswered questions. The explosion had shaken Aqualis and changed his life.

Tristan had a quick breakfast with his mother and Liam but needed answers about the explosion. He knew the official investigation would take a while and didn't want to wait. So, he put on his diving suit and headed to the port to gather information.

Walking through the streets of Aqualis, he noticed the tension in the air was tangible. People spoke in hushed tones, discussing their theories about what might have caused the explosion. Some blamed technical problems, while others suspected it was an act of sabotage.

Tristan was curious about the explosion on the Neptec Deep Tide during his visit to the port. As he made his way through the bustling port, he couldn't help but feel the tension in the air. The rivalry between Neptec and Aquadyne was well known at Aqualis, and it wasn't far-fetched that tensions between the two corporations had come to a head.

Tristan sought out old friends and acquaintances who worked on the Neptec Deep Tide. He wanted to hear firsthand what they had experienced and if they had noticed anything unusual before the explosion. As he chatted with them, he gathered details about what had happened on that fateful night.

One of his close friends, Alex, an engineer at Neptec's Deep Tide, confided in him about the strange behaviour he had noticed in some of the facility's systems in the days leading up to the explosion.

Reports of bugs and anomalies had increased, but management had dismissed the concerns as minor technical issues. Alex shared that he had even raised his concerns to management, but they brushed him off, saying they had everything under control.

Tristan listened closely as Alex recounted the incident. He felt a sense of unease wash over him, realising it might have been preventable. He made a mental note to continue his investigation and dig deeper.

"Something didn't add up, Tristan," Alex said quietly. "I don't think this was a simple accident. Someone knew what I was doing."

Alex's words echoed in Tristan's mind as he searched for answers. He began talking to other Deep Tide workers, gathering information and details about the weeks and days leading up to the explosion.

What he discovered left him even more uneasy: There were indications of an unusual increase in security activity at the facility.

With each clue he collected, Tristan became more convinced that the explosion had not been a simple accident. It seemed that there were elements of planning and premeditation involved. The idea of sabotage took hold in his mind, and he began to suspect a conspiracy.

He decided to take his findings to local authorities but was met with a cold reception when he showed up at the underwater investigations bureau.

The authorities seemed reluctant to accept the possibility of sabotage and were more interested in calming the concerned population than seeking the truth.

Frustrated and determined to move on, Tristan realised he must investigate independently. He had heard rumours about an underground network of rebels and ocean pirates operating in the shadows, defying corporations and fighting for justice and equality in the underwater world. Perhaps they could help him uncover the truth behind the explosion.

After searching the darkest areas of Aqualis, Tristan eventually encountered a contact who led him to a group of rebels known as "The Sons of the Abyss". They were diverse individuals who had sworn to fight corporate power and expose their darkest secrets.

Tristan met with the Children of the Abyss leader, an enigmatic woman named Mermaid. He told her his story and his suspicions about the explosion at Neptec's Deep Tide. Mermaid nodded solemnly and said to him:

"If you are willing to face the truth, you must be willing to go deep into the darkest depths of the ocean."

The rebel group offered to help him in the investigation and provided him with information on how to access the internal data of the corporations. Tristan immersed himself in the world of underwater hackers, learning how to navigate the advanced security technology of corporations and uncover hidden clues that could lead him to the truth.

As he deepened his search, Tristan realised that he was on a dangerous path and that powerful people would prefer the truth to remain hidden. But his determination did not waver. Neptec's Deep Tide explosion had changed his life forever, and he was willing to risk everything to find out who was behind that devastating act and why they had done it.

Chapter 5

CONFRONTATION WITH NEPTEC

Tristan delved into the digital maze of Neptec's systems, navigating layers of security and firewalls with the skill he had learned from the submarine rebels. He had uncovered several suspicious emails and internal communications that pointed to a possible conspiracy within the corporation. He was determined to find more evidence to support his sabotage theory in Neptec's Deep Tide explosion.

While scanning the archives for clues one night, he discovered a set of documents that caught his attention. They were technical reports detailing recurring problems at the Neptec facility in the weeks leading up to the explosion. The reports mentioned anomalies in security systems and some incidents that management overlooked or downplayed.

Tristan was reviewing one of these reports when he received an alert on his screen.

Someone had detected his presence in Neptec's system and was trying to track his location.

Wasting no time, he disconnected his equipment and prepared to flee.

As he hurriedly left the place, he realised he was being followed by two men dressed in black suits. The men quickly caught up with him and surrounded him.

"Who are you, and what are you doing here?" asked one of the men, his voice making it clear that he was unwilling to tolerate any evasion.

Tristan felt trapped, but his determination did not waver. He decided to be honest instead of trying to hide his intentions.

"I'm Tristan, an aquatic technician," he began, "and I'm investigating the explosion at Neptec's Deep Tide. I think it was sabotage, and I'm looking for evidence to support that theory."

The men exchanged fleeting glances and sinister smiles.

"Interesting, Tristan. We don't know where you got that idea, but it's completely wrong. It was an accident, and Neptec is working tirelessly to resolve it."

Tristan was not convinced. He had seen enough evidence to suggest otherwise, and his instinct told him these men were not what they seemed. However, he knew that he couldn't face them directly.

The men continued interrogating him to obtain information about his activities and connections with the

submarine rebels. Tristan managed to remain calm and give vague answers without revealing too much. But he knew his time was running out fast.

Finally, one of the men warned him with a stern and sombre tone, his words laced with a sense of urgency and concern, "Tristan, let me be unequivocally clear. Cease your investigations into this matter immediately. Neptec is a formidable corporate entity; you have no inkling of the formidable forces you're entangled with. If you persist in this pursuit, you're jeopardising yourself and those you hold dear. Your safety will be in jeopardy, and the consequences could be dire."

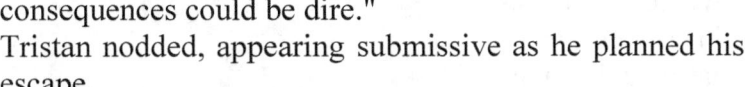

Tristan nodded, appearing submissive as he planned his escape.

He knew that he could not trust the word of these men and that his determination to uncover the truth about the explosion was stronger than ever.

After skilfully avoiding the Neptec operatives, Tristan swiftly submerged himself into the clandestine world of the submarine rebels, keen to tap into their wisdom and perspectives. He

vividly recounted his recent showdown with the Neptec enforcers, leaving nothing out as he shared the compelling evidence he'd uncovered.

Sirena, the chief of the enigmatic group known as the "Children of the Abyss," watched him intently, her expression a complex blend of empathy and fascination. Tristan, you are in a dangerous position," she warned him. "The men of Neptec will stop at nothing to protect their secrets. You must be cautious and ensure no one else knows what you're investigating."

Tristan understood the danger he was in, but he also knew he couldn't turn back. He had come too far in his search for answers and was determined to bring the truth to light.

In the following days, Tristan continued his investigation secretly, gathering more evidence suggesting a pattern of suspicious behaviour at Neptec. He spoke with workers at the facility who had noticed similar anomalies at other Deep Tides of the corporation. It seemed that something was happening in the shadows of Neptec, and Tristan was determined to find out what it was.

As he delved deeper into the conspiracy that had unleashed the explosion at Neptec's Deep Tide, he realised he was racing against time. The corporation's executives would stop at nothing to protect their secrets, and Tristan knew his life was in danger.

Chapter **6**

UNEXPECTED ALLIES

Tristan had been secretly investigating the explosion at Neptec's Deep Tide for weeks, facing hostility from corporate executives and growing danger. But his determination had not weakened, and his search for the truth led to an unexpected discovery that would change the course of his investigation.

On a fateful afternoon, as he delved deeper into the most obscure corners of the clandestine network, Tristan stumbled upon an encrypted message that seemed to hold vital information. The cryptic communication led him to a secluded, desolate spot in the ocean's abyss, where he was scheduled to rendezvous with a cadre of

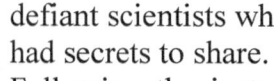

defiant scientists who had secrets to share.

Following the instructions, Tristan plunged into the dark waters and deep into a hidden cave. Upon reaching the cave's interior, he was greeted by a group of men and women wearing black diving suits and had a hard look on their faces. They were rebellious scientists who had worked on secret research projects for corporations and discovered dark secrets in the process.

During one fateful afternoon, as Tristan delved even further into the most shadowy recesses of the covert network, he serendipitously stumbled upon an encrypted message that appeared to house information of utmost importance. The enigmatic correspondence served as a guiding light, directing him to a remote, desolate location in the unfathomable depths of the ocean. He was slated to meet with a select group of renegade scientists, each harbouring their cache of closely guarded secrets, ready to be unveiled.

Dr Marcus leaned in, his expression grave, as he delivered his words with a sense of profound gravity. "The revelations we've uncovered are nothing short of staggering," he began, the weight of the information evident in his voice.

"These corporations aren't just after dominion over Deep Tides and the extraction of marine energy; they're also prepared to recklessly disrupt the delicate

ecological equilibrium of the ocean and jeopardise marine life, all in the relentless pursuit of corporate gains."

Tristan was impressed by the determination and bravery of this group of rebellious scientists.

As Tristan absorbed this startling revelation, he grasped the enormity of the risks they had all undertaken in exposing the unvarnished truth about the corporations. It became increasingly evident that their shared commitment to justice and transparency was a unifying force. A sense of unity began to emerge, and he recognised that they might wield the collective strength and resources needed to unearth and expose the intricate conspiracy that had instigated the devastating explosion at Neptec's Deep Tide facility.

The scientists shared their findings and evidence collected over the years with Tristan. They showed detailed reports on ocean chemical pollution, data on marine species' overexploitation, and testimonies of De ep Tides workers who had been threatened not to reveal the truth.

Tristan realised that these tests could be crucial to his research. Rebellious scientists also provided him access to a network of informants within corporations, people willing to risk everything to help expose the truth. Together, they began planning to reveal the corporate conspiracy to the world. They knew they would face fierce opposition, and their lives would be in danger, but they were willing to take that risk.

With each passing day, Tristan's sense of empowerment grew as he basked in the unwavering support of his newfound allies. He had discovered a band of like-minded individuals who were as devoted as he was to the cause of unravelling the truth and curbing the insatiable avarice of the corporations.

United by their common purpose, they coalesced into a potent and resolute team, standing prepared to confront whatever challenges lay ahead in their unwavering pursuit of their ultimate objective. As they planned their next move, Tristan realised he was uniquely positioned to change the course of history. Neptec's Deep Tide explosion had catalysed his search for truth, but what he had discovered since then was much bigger.

Chapter 7

THE PIRATES OF THE SEA

Tristan and the group of rebellious scientists led by Dr Marcus continued their search for evidence and evidence to expose the corporate conspiracy. Every day, they went deeper into a world of secrecy and corruption and knew they would face dangers and challenges on their way to the truth.

On a particular afternoon, during one of their exploratory missions in a secluded underwater expanse, Tristan and his comrades stumbled upon an unexpected sight. It wasn't the familiar vessels belonging to either of the two corporations. Instead, they found themselves face-to-face with a fleet of ships that bore the unmistakable mark of oceanic pirates. This notorious and elusive group had operated in the sea depths for an extended period.

These pirates were renowned for their audacious tactics and uncanny knack for navigating the underwater world while remaining virtually undetectable to corporations and local authorities. The leader of the pirates introduced himself as Captain Drake, an imposing man with a scar on his face and a sly look in his eyes.

When he learned that Tristan and his group were interested in the Deep Tides and exposing the illegal activities of corporations, he showed an unusually friendly interest.

"If they're looking for evidence against Neptec and Aquadyne, maybe we can help them," Captain Drake said, with a smile revealing a row of sharp teeth.

Dr Marcus and his fellow rebellious scientists exchanged sceptical glances as they observed the pirate leader closely. While harbouring reservations about placing complete trust in an individual with Captain Drake's reputation, they couldn't deny the potential value of his

extensive knowledge of the seas and his wealth of experience when confronting powerful corporations. Their collective understanding was that, despite the inherent risks, allying with Captain Drake might be a strategic move that could significantly aid their cause.

Tristan, for his part, was intrigued by the possibility that the pirates might have important information. He had learned to trust his instinct, which told him they should listen to what Captain Drake had to say.

With a calculated air of secrecy, the pirate leader disclosed that their covert network had been diligently surveilling the operations of Neptec and Aquadyne for an extended period, amassing a trove of potentially incriminating evidence against the corporations. Their surveillance efforts had unveiled a web of corruption, the ruthless exploitation of marine resources, and the deliberate acts of environmental contamination. Yet, despite this invaluable intelligence, they acknowledged their limitations—they lacked the necessary technological prowess and infrastructure to unveil this damning information to the world effectively.

Tristan and his group exchanged glances, acknowledging this could be a unique opportunity to obtain additional evidence to support their cause. Despite their reservations about pirates, they decided to collaborate as much as possible.

As they collaborated to amass the crucial information, Tristan's perspective shifted. He recognised that Captain Drake's pirate crew were far more than the unscrupulous criminals they were often portrayed as. They possessed a code of ethics and fervently believed in pursuing justice. It became increasingly evident that they were prepared to take a principled stand against the corporations, all to safeguard the beloved oceans and marine life they held so dearly. This revelation illuminated a shared commitment to a cause greater than themselves, uniting them in a common goal.

However, their collaboration did not go unnoticed. Neptec and Aquadyne began to suspect that something was happening in the ocean's depths and increased security at their facilities.

Tension grew as Tristan's group, and the pirates came closer to gathering the necessary evidence.

During a moonlit night, while they were in the thick of their covert operations, they suddenly found themselves ensnared in an ambush orchestrated by a squadron of heavily armed Neptec security submarines. The ensuing battle was nothing short of ferocious, with torpedoes and lasers streaking through the water in all directions, creating a dazzling display of combat beneath the waves. Tristan and his comrades exhibited unwavering valour, standing shoulder to shoulder with the pirates, but the odds were stacked against them as they found themselves outnumbered and outgunned.

In the heat of the ongoing skirmish, Captain Drake and Tristan came to a sobering realisation—they were locked in a deadlock with the Neptec forces. It was at this critical juncture that they made a daring and calculated choice.

Employing a swift, evasive manoeuvre, they broke free from their pursuers. They executed a skilful dive into the depths of a submarine canyon, expertly placing themselves beyond the grasp of their adversary's submarines.

Upon finally breaking through to the surface, they breathed a sigh of relief as the realisation dawned upon them that they had successfully eluded their relentless pursuers. However,

this hard-fought escape had come at a cost. Regrettably, both Tristan's group and the pirate crew had incurred casualties. Numerous members were nursing injuries, and Captain Drake bore a conspicuous wound on his arm as a testament to the rigours of the conflict they had just endured.

With a newfound sense of respect and camaraderie, the pirate leader fixed his gaze upon Tristan, his expression marked by admiration. "We've fought side by side, and the bonds we've forged in battle run deep,

"Captain Drake declared. "Our shared adversary unites us, and I anticipate our ongoing collaboration to further our mission of exposing the corporations and safeguarding our precious oceans. However, we must exercise even greater vigilance and readiness to face the challenges ahead."

With an unwavering nod of determination, Tristan signalled his commitment to the cause. Over time, he had come to respect the sea pirates and acknowledge that, despite their unorthodox approach, they were bound by a common aspiration for justice and transparency.

As a united front, they had braced themselves for any obstacle that might befall them in their relentless quest to unveil the truth about the enigmatic Deep Tides and the labyrinthine corporate conspiracy lurking beneath the ocean's surface.

Chapter **8**

THE UNDERWATER HACKER

Collaboration with the sea pirates led by Captain Drake had provided Tristan and his group with valuable information about the corporations' activities. However, they still needed more concrete evidence to expose the conspiracy behind Neptec's Deep Tide explosion. To get the necessary information, they decided to seek the help of an expert in underwater technology - an underwater hacker.

Within the underwater realm, hackers held a revered reputation for their unparalleled prowess in breaching formidable security systems that safeguarded the secrets of the deep sea. They constituted an

elusive, subaquatic force, a community of exceptional individuals characterised by their unyielding determination. Operating stealthily in the ocean's profound obscurity, they openly defied the supremacy of corporations and governments alike. Among their ranks, Tristan had often heard whispers of a legendary underwater hacker renowned by the moniker "Black Neptune."

This enigmatic figure was reputed to be the unparalleled virtuoso in his domain, celebrated as the preeminent mastermind in the art of subaquatic hacking.

With the help of Captain Drake's pirates, Tristan embarked on a quest to find Black Neptune. Navigating the perilous and shadowy expanse of the ocean, they embarked on an arduous quest, doggedly pursuing elusive traces and the hushed whispers of leads that might guide them to

their sought-after destination. After weeks of relentless investigation and traversing the abyssal waters, their tenacity was finally rewarded. A pivotal clue emerged, pointing them towards a desolate and secluded site near one of Aquadyne's Deep Tides. In this location, they hoped to unearth answers that had remained hidden for far too long.

With a sense of anticipation, Tristan and his resolute companions took the plunge, descending into the ocean's depths in a relentless pursuit of truth.

Their unwavering determination led them to discover a clandestine entrance concealed within the confines of an underwater cave, shrouded in mystique.

Venturing further into the subterranean passage, they came face to face with an enigmatic figure, a man cloaked in a sleek black diving suit. His visage remained concealed behind an inscrutable mask, and it was in that moment of revelation that they stood in the presence of none other than Black Neptune himself.

The enigmatic underwater hacker directed a scrutinising gaze towards Tristan and his accompanying group, with eyes that seemed capable of peering into their souls. In a measured, almost hushed tone, he finally broke the silence, his words carrying the weight of both wisdom and curiosity. "I've been apprised of your relentless quest for the elusive truth. What, I wonder, has led you to my doorstep?"

Tristan explained his mission and the need to obtain concrete evidence to expose the corporate conspiracy.

Acknowledging their mission with a profound understanding, Black Neptune nodded in agreement, signifying his willingness to contribute to their shared cause. He harboured no illusions about the perils of confronting powerful corporations; however, he remained steadfast in his conviction regarding the paramount significance of exposing the unvarnished truth to the world.

The underwater hacker disclosed that he had dedicated a substantial amount of time to monitoring the communications of the corporate behemoths. In doing so, he had unearthed a treasure trove of compelling evidence hinting at a covert rendezvous between the upper echelons of Neptec and Aquadyne. These clandestine meetings insinuated a collaborative endeavour of monumental proportions between the two corporate giants. Yet, the specifics of this project remained shrouded in obscurity, an enigma that continued to elude their grasp.

Recognising the gravity of their mission, Black Neptune readily consented to employ his unparalleled skills to infiltrate the innermost sanctums of corporate communication networks.

His primary aim was to procure unimpeachable data regarding the cryptic project that had ignited their curiosity. Yet, he issued a solemn caveat to his companions, underscoring the perils ahead. He stressed the imperative of evading detection at all costs, fully cognizant of the

treacherous terrain they were about to traverse. Tristan and his group were willing to take the risk. They realised they were entering dangerous territory but were determined to get to the bottom of the conspiracy and expose corporations for their actions. They began planning the operation together with Black Neptune. The undertaking of breaching the impregnable security systems of the corporations necessitated a synthesis of technical acumen and adept diving prowess. Tristan and his steadfast cohorts, bolstered by the indomitable spirit of Captain Drake's pirates, embarked on an arduous journey of intensive subaquatic training.

Their preparations encompassed a comprehensive regimen, equipping them with the essential skills required for this mission. To augment their capabilities, Black Neptune furnished them with a cache of specialised tools and state-of-the-art technology, each meticulously calibrated to facilitate their endeavour.

The fateful night of their operation descended upon them like a shroud of anticipation. With unwavering determination, Tristan and his resolute companions descended into the ocean's abyss, unwaveringly following the guidance of Black Neptune. They were armed with sophisticated camouflage devices, a vital arsenal in their clandestine mission, expertly designed to shield them from the prying eyes of corporate security cameras and surveillance systems. Every movement was tense, the water bearing down upon them, a palpable reminder of the perils that loomed as they stealthily closed in on their elusive target.

As they ventured further into the labyrinthine recesses of Neptec and Aquadyne's fortified security system, Tristan and his intrepid cohort began to fathom the sheer scale of the operation they had embarked upon.

The intricacies of the corporate defences unfurled before them like a complex puzzle, each layer revealing a new challenge to be overcome. There were layers and layers of protection and cutting-edge technology that they had to navigate. Black Neptune guided them through the intricate security mazes, eluding guards and overcoming obstacles.

After an arduous journey through the digital labyrinth of the corporate security system, they reached the apotheosis of their mission: a covert communications chamber concealed deep within the digital fortress. Here, they unearthed an extensive cache of records detailing clandestine meetings between the upper echelons of the corporate juggernauts. The evidence they uncovered was nothing short of staggering, painting a stark tableau of corporate collusion. The records indicated that these titans of industry were embroiled in a comprehensive project designed to extend their dominion over the Deep Tides, solidifying their stranglehold on the extraction of marine energy resources.

With a sense of urgency hanging in the air, Tristan swiftly set to work, capturing photographic evidence of the incriminating records. At the same time, Black Neptune employed his formidable skills to obliterate any trace of their intrusion from the tenacious security systems. Time was their greatest adversary; they understood that remaining in this precarious position was a gambit they could ill afford. Resolute, they knew their window of opportunity was limited, and they had to retrace their steps expeditiously, retracing their digital path back to the entry point before the relentless corporate sentinels closed in on their clandestine operation.

As they hurried out, they encountered a group of security guards. A confrontation broke out in the narrow and dark corridor.

The subaqueous skirmishes unfurled with an intensity that left little room for respite, as the

confined space placed combatants in close quarters. In this aquatic battleground, amidst the liquid embrace of the deep sea, each exchange of punches and kicks carried a weight far greater than the water's pressure.

Inseparable from the tempestuous fray, Tristan and his dedicated companions displayed unwavering valour, their commitment to the cause burning brightly in the subaqueous darkness. Shoulder to shoulder, they fought gallantly, a dynamic alliance forged through shared determination and a common objective. Alongside the indomitable forces of Black Neptune and the audacious pirates under Captain Drake's command, they rallied with tenacity and resourcefulness.

After an arduous struggle, they eventually triumphed over the tenacious corporate sentinels, though not without their share of battle scars. The physical toll of the confrontation was evident as they navigated their escape from the oppressive clutches of the corporations' fortified installation.

With their hard-fought prize in hand - the crucial evidence they had sought - they plunged into the expansive open waters, distancing themselves from the enemy's stronghold.

Their mission had been accomplished, but the steep cost was undeniable, etched into their very beings as a testament to their unwavering determination.

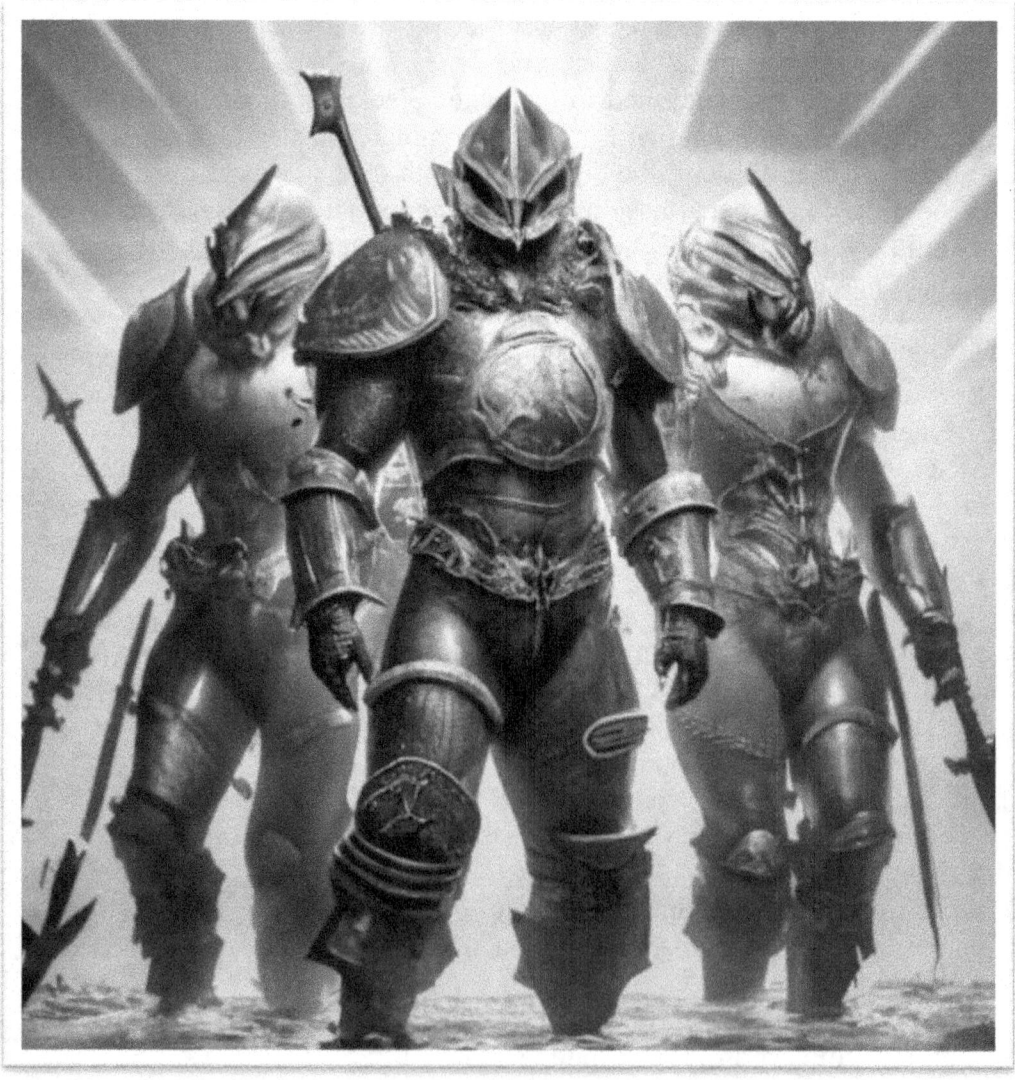

Chapter **9**

BETRAYAL IN THE DEEP

Tristan and his group had obtained concrete evidence of a corporate conspiracy to expand their control over the Deep Tides and monopolise marine energy extraction. The operation of infiltrating the security systems of the corporations had been risky, but they had succeeded and were closer than ever to exposing the truth.

In the quiet hours following the operation, as they huddled together in their secure hideout, the group faced an unforeseen and treacherous turn of events. It was a night that would be etched into their memories as Evelyn, a trusted comrade who had fought alongside them in the daring mission, revealed her shocking act of betrayal. Her allegiance had shifted, aligning with the corporations they had strived to expose. She had clandestinely forged an alliance with Neptec and Aquadyne, relinquishing critical information regarding the whereabouts of Tristan and the entire group.

The revelation of this betrayal casts a shadow of doubt and suspicion over their tight-knit band of rebels, leaving them grappling with the profound implications of Evelyn's actions.

Evelyn's betrayal reverberated through the group like a seismic shock, leaving them in disbelief and deep emotional turmoil. The bonds of trust that had been painstakingly forged among these allies were now shattered, and they grappled with the painful realisation that someone they had considered a steadfast friend had chosen to barter their loyalty to the corporations they had dedicated themselves to opposing. The sense of betrayal cut deep, and the group questioned their judgment, the essence of their mission, and the values they held dear. The fallout of this shocking revelation would test the group's resilience and unity as they sought to navigate the treacherous waters ahead.

Evelyn had been a steadfast member of their group since its inception, standing shoulder-to-shoulder with them in their shared pursuit of justice and transparency.

Her unwavering commitment to the cause reassured everyone and fostered a sense of unity and trust among the allies. None of them had harboured even the slightest inkling that she could be capable of such treachery. She had been a confidant, a companion, and a symbol of solidarity within their ranks, and her betrayal felt like a profound breach of faith that sent shockwaves through the group, causing them to reassess their ability to discern

friend from foe in the complex and perilous world of underwater intrigue.

Tristan was overwhelmed by Evelyn's betrayal. He had trusted her and shared sensitive information about the operation. Now, their lives were in danger, and the evidence they had collected could be in the hands of corporations.

Tristan was overwhelmed by Evelyn's betrayal. He had trusted her and shared sensitive information about the operation. Now, their lives were in danger, and the evidence they had collected could be in the hands of corporations.

As the revelation of Evelyn's betrayal still hung heavily in the air, a sudden and unexpected threat closed in on them. A rapid encirclement of Neptec and Aquadyne's security forces had their haven surrounded. Panic began to set in, and desperation filled the room. The gravity of their predicament became all too apparent as they found themselves in a perilous standoff, cut off from escape and surrounded by the very entities they had been tirelessly working to expose. In a chilling moment of revelation, the security team leader, Donovan, approached the captured group, wearing a self-satisfied smile. His words cut through the tension like a knife, "We had a front-row informant," he gloated, approvingly glancing at Evelyn, who stood there, seemingly without remorse.

Her betrayal had served as the perfect opening for the corporations, and they now held the upper hand, their victory within reach. It was a bitter pill to swallow as the group realised that their every move had been anticipated and their plans had been cleverly unravelled by the person they had once trusted.

Evelyn looked at Tristan and the group with remorse before speaking. "I'm sorry," he murmured. "I had no choice.

They threatened to harm my family if I didn't cooperate."

Tristan was overwhelmed by a mixture of anger and betrayal. He knew Evelyn was trapped in a difficult situation, but he still couldn't forgive his actions. The betrayal of someone they trusted had endangered their lives and their mission.

Donovan, with a sense of authority that sent shivers down the spines of the captured group, barked orders to his subordinates.

Disarmed and surrounded by corporate security, the group members were handcuffed and led away to a waiting convoy, which would transport them to a high-security Neptec facility. Evelyn, their former ally turned traitor, was granted a false sense of belonging as she walked alongside the security team of Neptec and Aquadyne, her once-familiar comrades now donning the uniforms of the very corporations they had sought to expose. The situation

was dire, and the battle for truth had taken a disheartening turn.

At the Neptec facility, Tristan and the others were held in individual cells. They were separated and without access to their communications. They knew they had to act quickly to escape and prevent the evidence they had obtained from falling into the hands of corporations. Tristan and Dr Marcus devised an escape plan.

They used their technical skills and knowledge of underwater technology to turn off the facility's security system temporarily.

They took advantage of a limited time window to free themselves from their cells and meet at a pre-arranged meeting point.

The escape had been a harrowing experience, fraught with danger at every turn. They had navigated labyrinthine corridors and bypassed high-tech security measures, always one step ahead of their corporate captors. Their unwavering determination and the seamless coordination of their efforts allowed them to outsmart the security guards and make their way out of the facility's confines.

Now, deep in the heart of the ocean, they found themselves beyond the immediate reach of their pursuers, but the shadow of Neptec and Aquadyne loomed large. They knew they were still being hunted; their every move was monitored by the corporations they had dared to challenge. Their quest for justice and the revelation of the corporate conspiracy had become a high-stakes game of cat and mouse, with the odds heavily stacked against them.

While hiding from the corporations' search teams, Tristan and the others realised that Evelyn's betrayal had brought to light an even darker part of the conspiracy. They knew they had to stop corporations before they carried out their project and jeopardised the ocean's ecological balance.

Meeting at their meeting place, Tristan and the group planned their next move.

Realising the need for more substantial evidence and a comprehensive strategy to unveil the

corporations to the global audience, they were consumed by an unwavering determination to unearth the masterminds behind the conspiracy. Their resolve extended beyond mere revelation; they aspired to unmask the true architects of this clandestine operation, assigning names and faces to those who had triggered the explosion at Neptec, thus endangering the very foundation of the underwater world.

Their pursuit had morphed into an all-consuming obsession for Tristan and his comrades.

They were prepared to stake everything, even their very lives, to serve the cause of justice and unveil the intricate web of deceit that menaced the equilibrium of the oceans and the cherished marine life they held dear. Each of them bore the heavy burden of responsibility, driven by an imminent sense of purpose, fully aware that time was of the essence and the implications of their battle would impact not only their destinies but also the fate of the entire underwater realm and, ultimately, that of the surface world.

Evelyn's shocking betrayal had undoubtedly dealt a devastating blow to the group, shattering the trust they had once placed in her. However, far from deterring them, it ignited an even fiercer determination within Tristan and his companions. This treachery only fuelled their unwavering commitment to confront the formidable corporations and reveal the sinister conspiracy that loomed menacingly, threatening to cast the underwater world into the clutches of unbridled avarice and ruination.

With a renewed resolve, they stood shoulder to shoulder, more resolute than ever, prepared to challenge the indomitable forces that sought to perpetuate the oppression and deceit. Their mission was no longer a mere quest but an ardent crusade for justice, transparency, and preserving the marine world they held dear. The undeniable gravity of their endeavour impelled them forward, for they recognised that their actions would not only shape their destinies but also bear profound consequences for the entire underwater domain and, in the broader scheme of things, the world above the surface.

Chapter 10

THE LOST TECHNOLOGY

After escaping the Neptec and Aquadyne facility and facing Evelyn's betrayal, Tristan and his group find themselves in a precarious situation. Despite obtaining concrete evidence of the corporate conspiracy, they were in exile, hiding from the security teams relentlessly pursuing them.

As they formulated their forthcoming strategy, Tristan carefully reflected on the evidence they had secured and the enigmatic nature of the underlying conspiracy. While it was evident that the corporations were engaged in a collaborative project to extend their dominance over the Deep Tides, there remained critical gaps in their understanding. The missing fragments of information weighed heavily on Tristan's thoughts, compelling him to delve deeper into the matter.

He was convinced that there was an elusive, yet pivotal, component that still eluded their grasp, one that held the potential to unravel the full extent of the conspiracy.

It was the missing puzzle piece, the key to comprehending the true scale of the scheme that had drawn them into a perilous web of intrigue.

This realisation galvanised their determination, as they knew that uncovering this hidden truth was essential for their quest and the future of the submerged world and the world above the ocean's surface.

While immersed in thought one night, Tristan recalled a conversation with Black Neptune, the underwater hacker, during his infiltration operation at corporate facilities.

The underwater hacker had alluded to the presence of advanced marine technology that had remained concealed for an extended period. Initially, Tristan hadn't given this revelation much thought, but with the mounting gravity of their situation, it had gradually grown in significance within his mind. He now firmly believed that this mysterious technology was the elusive fragment that would complete the intricate puzzle of the conspiracy.

It held the promise of unveiling not only the extent of corporate machinations but also the potential to reshape the future of the underwater world, making it a beacon of hope and progress rather than a pawn in the hands of greedy corporations.

He decided it was time to investigate further. He contacted Black Neptune through secure communication and asked about the advanced marine technology he mentioned. The underwater hacker explained that it was a long-lost technology called "Project Leviathan."

Project Leviathan, Tristan learned, was a collaborative endeavour between scientists and technologists aiming to craft a pioneering marine technology capable of sustainably harnessing the boundless energy of the ocean, heralding an era of perpetual and clean power supply. This breakthrough held the promise of reshaping the world by eliminating the dire reliance on finite fossil fuels and offering an abundant, eco-conscious, unending energy source.

The implications of such technology were staggering, painting a vision of a world that had transcended the pollution and depletion associated with traditional energy sources.

However, the Leviathan Project had been kept secret due to the greed of corporations and their desire to maintain control over marine energy extraction.

They had concealed this advanced technology's existence and continued exploiting conventional marine resources for their benefit.

Tristan's epiphany was that Project Leviathan held the crux of the corporate conspiracy. He recognised that unveiling this long-lost technology could be a game-changer. It could endow them with the means to confront the corporations substantially and effectively. Furthermore, it could offer a sustainable resolution to the worldwide energy dilemma, profoundly altering the current landscape.

Black Neptune extended his assistance, proposing to aid Tristan and his team in tracing the whereabouts of Project Leviathan.

He acknowledged the daunting challenge ahead, recognising that the corporations had spared no effort to conceal its existence. Nevertheless, they were prepared to stake everything on this mission.

Together, they began investigating clues and records that could lead them to Project Leviathan.

As they delved deeper into their search, they discovered information suggesting the lost technology was hidden in a remote, highly protected location in the ocean's depths.

Tristan and his team, accompanied by Black Neptune, undertook a perilous mission to locate

Project Leviathan. Their journey led them through uncharted waters, fraught with numerous challenges. Over weeks, they diligently pursued the leads and clues left behind by the scientists who had contributed to the project many decades ago.

Finally, they reached a remote location in the ocean abyss, where they found what they had been looking for. A series of advanced

and technologically impressive underwater structures towered over the sea. It was Project Leviathan.

The structures they sought were concealed beneath layers of algae and vibrant corals, a testimony to the passage of time. Remarkably, these structures still held their functionality, standing as silent witnesses to the past.

With his remarkable skills, Black Neptune initiated the process of infiltrating the security systems guarding the long-forgotten Leviathan Project. They aimed to unveil this hidden technology and expose the corporations' concealed agenda.

The news of advanced marine technology hidden for so long spread rapidly, causing a global shock. Society realised that there was a sustainable alternative to marine energy extraction that corporations had been deliberately hiding.

The Neptec and Aquadyne corporations' exposure left them in a precarious position. The revelation of the Leviathan Project acted as a catalyst, igniting widespread protests and inviting global scrutiny into the activities of these corporate giants in the depths of the oceans.

The top executives found themselves in the eye of an escalating storm of public outrage and government pressure. Public opinion and governmental actions were turning decisively against them, making it a turning point in the battle for justice and transparency.

Tristan, his group, and Black Neptune had made significant progress in their struggle for justice and truth. They discovered and revealed advanced marine technology that had the potential to change the world and end the ruthless exploitation of the oceans.

Chapter **11**

THE ULTIMATUM

The revelation of the Leviathan Project had brought to light the truth about corporations and their conspiracy to expand their control over the Deep Tides. Society was shocked and enraged, and corporations were under intense public and government scrutiny. Tristan and his group's struggle for justice and truth was bearing fruit, but the consequences were becoming increasingly serious.

One morning, while Tristan and the others were discussing their next move in their hidden shelter, they received an unexpected communication.

It was a direct message from senior executives at Neptec and Aquadyne. The corporations had issued an ultimatum.

The message sent was unequivocal and carried ominous undertones. The corporations demanded the unconditional

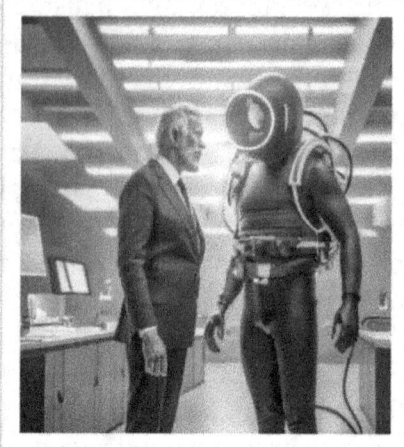

surrender of Tristan and his group, making it clear that defiance would come at a high cost. In exchange for surrender, they offered a conditional assurance: they would refrain from immediate public retaliation and grant the group the opportunity to depart the submerged world without disturbance.

However, they made it a point to underscore the gravity of the situation, emphasising that refusal would bring severe repercussions. Among these consequences were the persistent pursuit and unrelenting persecution of the group, coupled with the menacing threat of exposing their identities to the world. The ultimatum presented Tristan with a momentous decision that would shape the course of their struggle for justice.

Tristan and the others looked at the message in disbelief. They knew corporations were desperate to regain control of the situation, but they did not expect such a direct and threatening ultimatum. The decision before them was terrifying and fraught with risk.

As they debated their answer, Tristan realised he was at a crossroads. On the one hand, surrendering would mean abandoning their fight for justice and allowing corporations to continue their ruthless exploitation of the oceans. On the other hand, rejecting the ultimatum would mean facing even more intense persecution and exposing oneself to grave dangers.

Dr Marcus, the perennial voice of prudence and wisdom, vehemently opposed the notion of surrender. "Turning back now is not an option," he declared with unflinching resolve. "Our journey has been marked by challenges, and we understood the risks and inevitable consequences from the outset. However, we cannot forsake our noble cause. To capitulate would be a betrayal of all those who vested their trust in us, and we would have failed not only ourselves but an entire world that hungers for the truth." Dr Marcus's impassioned plea echoed within the hearts of Tristan and the group, reinforcing their commitment to their chosen path.

Tristan agreed with Dr Marcus but also understood the situation's gravity. I knew they had to decide and be prepared to face the consequences.

They sent a message in response to the ultimatum, in which they rejected surrender and affirmed their commitment to exposing truth and justice in the underwater world. They knew this decision would put their lives in imminent danger.

Shortly after sending their response, the corporations went public with their intention to expose Tristan and his group. They published their identities and false accusations in the media, portraying them as dangerous criminals who threatened the safety of the underwater world.

Society was divided. Some believed the accusations of the corporations and considered Tristan and his group a threat. Others saw corporations as the real villains and supported the pursuit of justice.

The persecution of Tristan and his group reached a fevered pitch. The persecution of Tristan and his group reached a fevered pitch. They found themselves relentlessly pursued by tenacious corporate security teams, their every move shadowed by imminent danger. The once tranquil underwater society now teetered on the brink of chaos, and the battle for justice had escalated to a desperate and harrowing struggle. The world beneath the waves had become a relentless battleground, with Tristan and his companions fighting against all odds to bring their mission to fruition.

Tristan was under overwhelming pressure. He knew he had made the right decision in rejecting the ultimatum, but he also understood the personal cost he was paying. He was willing to risk his life for what he believed in, but he also worried about the safety of his family and friends.

One night, as they huddled together in the shelter's dimly lit confines, Tristan couldn't help but reflect on the difficult and often heart-wrenching choices he'd been forced to make throughout

his unyielding pursuit of justice. These decisions bore heavily on his conscience, and he felt the immense responsibility that had fallen squarely on his shoulders. With every step they took in their perilous journey, Tristan questioned the path they had chosen and its toll on each group member. The sea's depths held both their dreams and their nightmares, and Tristan grappled with the tremendous burden of leadership and the choices that could ultimately shape their fate.

At that moment, he received an unexpected message. It was from someone who called himself "The Unknown Ally." The message claimed that this person had vital information to help Tristan and his group fight against

corporations. They offered to meet in a safe place and reveal the information.

Tristan shared the news with Dr Marcus and the others. Despite their scepticism about the identity of the "unknown ally," they were willing to investigate any opportunity that might help their cause.

They encountered the "unknown ally" in a remote and well-protected location. The person was revealed to be a former high-level Neptec executive who had been involved in the conspiracy of corporations and had decided to step forward to reveal the truth.

The former executive provided additional evidence that confirmed the conspiracy of the corporations and the depth of their corruption.

He also revealed information about the location of secret documents that could be the key to exposing the royal leaders.

Recognising the immense value and potential peril of the information they had uncovered, Tristan and his steadfast group began deliberating on the most strategic way to leverage it. They knew that this knowledge had the power to expose the true culprits behind the corporate conspiracy and ultimately hold them accountable. In the dimly lit chamber of their secret hideout, they planned an audacious operation, meticulously analysing each step with unwavering determination. The mission was not just about gathering evidence; it was a decisive move that could bring the shadowy orchestrators of the conspiracy into the unforgiving light of justice. The weight of the impending operation was palpable, but they were resolute in their resolve to see it through.

Chapter 12

THE BATTLE IN THE DEEP

The revelation of the Leviathan Project and the refusal of Tristan and his group to surrender had brought the struggle for justice and truth in the ocean's depths to the point of no return. The corporations had launched a fierce counterattack, relentlessly pursuing Tristan and his allies. Underwater society was divided, some supporting their cause and others believing the corporations' false accusations.

The chase peaked when corporate forces located the location of Tristan and his group's underwater shelter. Battle seemed inevitable, and Tristan and the others prepared to face their pursuers bravely.

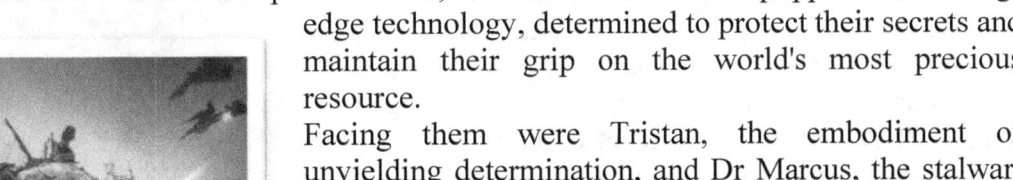

The fierce confrontation erupted in the profound depths of the ocean, where the unrelenting water pressure and the encompassing darkness added an extra layer of complexity to the already daunting challenge.

On one side were the formidable corporate forces, armed to the teeth and equipped with cutting-edge technology, determined to protect their secrets and maintain their grip on the world's most precious resource.

Facing them were Tristan, the embodiment of unyielding determination, and Dr Marcus, the stalwart voice of reason, along with their unwavering allies. The scene was nothing short of an epic showdown, a battle that would determine the immediate outcome, the fate of the submerged world, and the pursuit of justice that had brought them all to this pivotal moment. The clash of forces in the watery abyss was a testament to the human spirit's resilience and the quest for truth and equality.

The fighting was fierce and chaotic. Rays of underwater energy illuminated the dark abyss, and explosions echoed in the water. Tristan and the others fought bravely, using their wits and skills to overcome their opponents. Guerrilla tactics and underwater mobility gave them a head start.

Captain Drake and his sea pirates joined the battle, drawing on their ocean knowledge and experience in naval engagements. His combat skills and boldness were invaluable to Tristan and his group.

The underwater battle raged on for hours, an unrelenting struggle that pitted the indomitable determination of both sides against each other. The corporate forces were unwavering in their resolve to halt Tristan and his allies, clinging to their secrets with unyielding tenacity. On the other side, Tristan and his comrades were equally resolute, their determination driven by their unwavering commitment to safeguard the truth and to ensure that justice prevailed. The

relentless combat beneath the waves was a testament to the unending battle between the forces of greed and the unwavering pursuit of transparency and equality. This battle would leave an indelible mark on the submerged world.

During the battle, Tristan came face to face with Donovan, Neptec's security leader and one of the main enemies.

Donovan had a look of relentless determination in his eyes and was determined to capture Tristan. The fight between Tristan and Donovan was intense. Punches and kicks were thrown underwater, demonstrating their skill in underwater combat. Tristan knew that this battle was personal and that he had to defeat Donovan to protect his group and his cause.

After an intense and relentless struggle, Tristan finally gained the upper hand in his battle against Donovan, delivering a decisive blow that rendered the corporate enforcer unconscious. The taste of this momentary triumph filled him with a surge of newfound energy and

unwavering determination. However, Tristan remained acutely aware that this was merely a battle within a much larger war, and the fight was far from its conclusion.

The fighting continued as the corporate forces and Tristan and his allies engaged in a battle of wills and abilities. Explosions and beams of underwater energy illuminated the abyss as the battle intensified. Finally, after hours of fighting, the corporate forces began to retreat. They suffered significant casualties and could not continue the battle without risking more resources and personnel. The momentary victory belonged to Tristan and his allies.

The battle in the depths had served as a crucible of valour and unwavering resolve. Tristan and his steadfast group had resolutely demonstrated their readiness to confront adversity and surmount any obstacle in their relentless pursuit of justice and enlightenment in the submerged realm. They had fearlessly challenged the

formidable might of the corporations, championed their deeply held convictions and proved their indomitable courage.

Following the gruelling battle, Tristan and his companions returned to their underwater refuge, marked by exhaustion but tinged with triumph. The realisation was that the ongoing conflict loomed large; the corporations were far from conceding defeat. Nevertheless, their resolve had been unyielding, and their capacity to confront adversaries of significant influence had been resoundingly established.

Chapter 13

REVELATION

After the epic battle in the ocean's depths, Tristan and his group returned exhausted to their underwater shelter. They had temporarily defeated the corporate forces but knew the fighting was far from over. The consequences of their confrontation had resonated in underwater society, and the divide between those who supported them and those who believed the false accusations of corporations had deepened.

As they recovered from the battle, Tristan and the others realised they had reached a critical point in their quest for justice and truth. They needed to expose the true extent of the corporate conspiracy and the implications of the advanced marine technology they had discovered.

To do this, they decided to use the information provided by the former high-level executive of Neptec. This individual had access to secret documents detailing the plans of the corporations and the people behind the conspiracy.

Tristan and his group gathered inside their underwater shelter in a secure communications room. With Black Neptune in charge of communication security, they began examining the documents provided by the former executive.

The documents unveiled the staggering dimensions of the conspiracy. Neptec and Aquadyne had joined forces in a covert endeavour named "Operation Trident." They aimed to extend their dominion over the Deep Tides, securing unrestricted access to worldwide marine energy extraction facilities. Their scheme involved the monopolisation of marine energy extraction, including the elimination of any potential competitors.

Furthermore, the documents unveiled the true identities of the masterminds behind Neptec and Aquadyne. These were formidable, ruthless figures who had clandestinely manoeuvred for

decades. They were prepared to utilise the advanced marine technology of Project Leviathan to fulfil their objectives, regardless of the consequences for the ocean and humanity.

The most shocking revelation was the true nature of Project Leviathan. It was an advanced marine energy extraction technology and an underwater weapon of mass destruction. Corporations had developed a way to turn ocean energy into a powerful weapon capable of devastating underwater cities.

Tristan and his companions were deeply shaken by the potential devastation Project Leviathan could bring about. They recognised the urgent n eed to prevent this technology from falling into the hands of corporations, as it posed a severe threat to the underwater world, one that could lead to catastrophic consequences if not thwarted.

They decided that the disclosure of this information was vital to their cause. They were to expose the true extent of the conspiracy and the implications of advanced marine technology to win the support of underwater society and pressure corporations to stop their plans.

Tristan and his group communicated with allies in the underwater society who had been following their fight. They decided to organise an underwater press conference in a secure location and use it to reveal the information they had di scovered.

The press conference was a major event held in a large underwater chamber. Underwater media cameras and journalists gathered to hear the revelations from Tristan and his group.

Tristan stepped forward and courageously revealed the full extent of the corporate conspiracy, shedding light on the ominous implications of the advanced marine technology. He stressed the dire consequences this technology could bring, potentially destroying the underwater world they cherished. With unwavering determination, he implored the underwater society to come together and join forces to counteract the corporations, safeguard their homes, and preserve the sanctity of the ocean. The press conference had an immediate impact.

Underwater society was shocked by the revelation and the magnitude of the threat. Many who had doubted Tristan and his group now joined their cause, seeing them as advocates for justice and the environment.

The Neptec and Aquadyne corporations found themselves in an increasingly precarious situation. The revelation of their clandestine agendas and the advanced marine technology placed them under severe scrutiny from government authorities and the general public. The enigmatic leaders behind these powerful entities became primary targets for investigation and global attention.

Tristan and his group had made significant progress in their fight for justice and truth in the underwater world. They had revealed the true extent of the corporate conspiracy and the implications of advanced marine technology. As they prepared for the challenges that still awaited them, they knew they had to maintain their resolve and move forward in their quest for justice and ocean protection.

Chapter 14

THE ESCAPE

The public revelation of the corporate conspiracy and Project Leviathan's true nature profoundly impacted underwater society. Outrage and support for Tristan and his group grew as the truth emerged. However, they had also attracted the relentless attention of corporations Neptec and Aquadyne, who were determined to stop them at all costs.

The unveiling of the true corporate leaders and the revelation of their advanced marine technology triggered a wave of intense government and public scrutiny. Underwater authorities initiated a crackdown on Neptec and Aquadyne, but the corporate leaders were unwavering in their resolve to apprehend Tristan and his group and reclaim their lost dominion. Their determination to regain control was unwavering, and the underwater world teetered on the precipice of a monumental showdown. Tristan and the others realised they were in a precarious situation.

Corporate forces had intensified their pursuit, and they found it increasingly difficult to move freely in the underwater world. They knew they had to take drastic measures to protect themselves and continue their fight for justice and truth.

The decision was clear that they must flee and seek refuge in the ocean's depths, where corporate forces would struggle to find them. Escape would be dangerous and full of challenges, but it was the only option they had to survive and continue their fight.

Tristan and his companions painstakingly readied themselves for their escape. They stockpiled supplies, weaponry, and survival equipment, fully aware that they might encounter unforeseen challenges in the profound depths of the ocean. Their preparations needed to cover a spectrum of potential eventualities as the path ahead was uncertain.

Black Neptune put his formidable hacking skills to work, expertly diverting the attention of corporate forces while simultaneously creating clever diversions. These tactics effectively cloaked their escape, allowing them to slip away without detection.

It was arduous and dangerous, but Black Neptune was an expert in the digital underwater world and knew how to circumvent corporate surveillance.

The night of the flight came quickly. Tristan and his group plunged into the dark, cold waters of the ocean, following a carefully planned route that would take them to unknown depths and remote places where they could find shelter.

The initial hours of their escape were fraught with tension and anxiety. Every sound, every ripple in the water, and every movement seemed like a potential harbinger of danger. Corporate forces were operating at maximum vigilance, actively scouring the underwater world in their relentless pursuit of Tristan and his group.

As they advanced in their escape, they encountered various daunting challenges. Hostile sea creatures lurked in their path, necessitating the use of their survival skills and equipment to fend off these aquatic adversaries.

Moreover, they grappled with the formidable challenges of underwater navigation, where darkness and immense water pressure bore down upon them with unwavering intensity.

The search for shelter led them to a labyrinth of underwater caves in the ocean's depths. It was a dark and mysterious place, far removed from civilisation and the reach of corporate forces. They set up their new shelter in one of the largest and safest caves, where they could hide and plan their next moves.

As they settled into their new refuge, Tristan and the others reflected on the cost of their struggle for justice and truth. They sacrificed their security and former lives to stand up to powerful corporations. Although safer in the ocean's depths, they knew they could not turn back.

Underwater society remained divided, some supporting their cause and others still influenced by the corporations' false accusations.

Tristan and his group understood that they must continue their struggle and find a way to fully expose the truth and stop the plans of the corporations.

Black Neptune continued its work on the underwater digital network, gathering additional information about the activities of corporations and their actual leaders. They knew they needed solid evidence to bring to the authorities and the public, and they were willing to risk everything to get it.

The escape of Tristan and his group marked the inauguration of a new phase in their relentless battle for justice and truth within the underwater world. The hurdles and perils encountered in the ocean's depths only served to fortify their resolve further. Driven by their unwavering belief in the righteousness of their cause, they remained steadfast in their determination to safeguard the ocean and the underwater society from the relentless grasp of unscrupulous corporations.

Chapter 15

THE SECRET REFUGE

Tristan and his group had escaped the relentless clutches of the Neptec and Aquadyne corporations. They had dived into the ocean's depths in search of shelter, where corporate forces would struggle to find them. The escape had been dangerous and full of challenges, but they had reached a remote and mysterious place where they could plan their next move.

This clandestine sanctuary was concealed within an enigmatic underwater grotto nestled in the profound recesses of the ocean. They embarked on a treacherous odyssey through a complex network of underwater corridors to gain entry, confronting the foreboding shroud of darkness and relentless water pressure.

Their arduous journey culminated in a crevice within the ocean floor, granting them passage to the cavern's entrance.

The entrance to the cavern was hidden behind a curtain of seaweed, making it almost invisible to anyone passing by.

Tristan and the others carefully swam through the algae and entered the cavern, relieved they had found a haven.

Upon crossing the threshold into the cavern's concealed embrace, they activated their underwater lights, dispelling the shadowy enigma that had veiled the space. The cavern unfurled its wide expanse before them, unveiling a surreal tapestry of peculiar, vibrant rock formations. Underwater stalactites and stalagmites adorned the cavern, ascending majestically from its floor and gracefully from its ceiling, instilling a profound sense of beauty and awe within the explorers.

Tristan and the others began to explore the cavern in search of a suitable place to establish their shelter. Finally, they found a safe and protected area inside the cavern, where the roof was raised enough for everyone to settle comfortably.

With its expertise in underwater technology, Black Neptune began installing security and communications systems to protect its secret shelter.

He used his hacking skills to create a digital shield that would make it difficult for corporate forces to track his location.

Meanwhile, Dr Marcus and the others took it upon themselves to gather food and resources from the underwater environment. The cavern was teeming with marine life, and they could collect algae and fish to ensure their survival in the refuge.

As they settled into their new underwater home, Tristan and the others began planning their next move. They knew they should use the information they had revealed at the press conference to pressure the authorities and the public to act against the corporations.

Black Neptune persisted in his tireless efforts within the underwater digital network, unearthing further evidence of the corporations' activities and revealing the true identities of their leaders.

Whenever he stumbled upon valuable information, he relayed it to Tristan and the rest of the group. They dedicated themselves diligently to cataloguing, refining, and framing the data, preparing it for a compelling presentation.

The concealed refuge became their sanctuary, granting them the invaluable resources and solitude required for extensive preparation and strategic contemplation. Fully aware that the corporate enforcers would persistently hunt them, they recognised the necessity of cleverness and resolute determination in their ongoing crusade for justice and truth.

Amid the perpetual darkness of their submerged sanctuary, Tristan engaged in profound introspection. He contemplated the profound commitment he and his companions had invested in their cause. Sacrificing their former lives and confronting innumerable perils, they remained resolute in their unwavering mission to secure justice and safeguard the vast expanse of the ocean. Rather than deterring them, the trials and sacrifices had only fortified their determination to persevere.

Dr Marcus shared his optimism and determination. "We have come too far to turn back," he reminded them. "Our cause is just and necessary, and we must continue to fight for what we believe in."

As their plans progressed, Tristan and the others realised they needed allies in their fight.

In their quest to build a formidable movement for ocean protection and justice, Tristan and his group actively networked with like-minded individuals and factions within the underwater society. They recognised that confronting the might of powerful corporations demanded a united front, requiring the collaboration of individuals and groups who held a steadfast commitment to preserving the ocean. Together, they sought to consolidate their efforts, pooling their resources and resolve to amplify their collective impact.

While exploring the cavern's winding passages, Tristan and Dr Marcus stumbled upon enigmatic inscriptions etched into the cavern walls.

These cryptic marks, aged by centuries, piqued their curiosity and drew them into the depths of an intriguing historical puzzle. The inscriptions hinted at a forgotten civilisation or culture that had once thrived beneath the ocean's surface, leaving behind a legacy of secrets waiting to be unravelled.

As Tristan and Dr Marcus closely scrutinised the inscriptions, the ancient symbols gradually revealed their

profound message. The writings conveyed a sense of urgency, emphasising the paramount significance of safeguarding the ocean's delicate balance.

They bore witness to the wisdom drawn from marine nature, serving as both a cautionary tale and a poignant reminder of humanity's duty to act as stewards of the deep.

The inscriptions beckoned to them as an age-old plea for preserving the ocean's splendour and the importance of living in harmony with its intricate ecosystems.

The discovery of these ancient inscriptions deep within the cavern profoundly impacted Tristan and Dr Marcus. They interpreted the symbols as a powerful sign, affirming that their pursuit of justice and truth was aligned with an enduring wisdom that transcended generations. The inscriptions served as a wellspring of inspiration, invigorating their unwavering dedication to their cause.

It was as if the ocean had spoken to them through the language of the ages, urging them to persevere in their quest to protect and preserve its irreplaceable beauty and ecological harmony.

The secret shelter in the underwater cavern symbolised the determination of Tristan and his party. They were willing to face any challenge and overcome any obstacle in their quest for justice and ocean protection.

As they continued to plan and prepare, they knew that their struggle was far from over and that they would face even greater challenges in the future.

Chapter **16**

THE BETRAYAL OF A FRIEND

The underwater cavern had become Tristan and his group's secret refuge, where they could plan their next move in their fight for justice and truth in the underwater world. As the days passed, they worked hard to gather additional evidence of the corporations' activities and to seek allies in their cause.

In the relentless battle for justice and the protection of the ocean, Tristan and his steadfast allies had forged a bond that went beyond friendship, rooted in shared values and an unwavering determination. They had become a united front, their spirits unyielding in the face of the corporate conspiracy. Their unity was a beacon of hope in the ocean's depths, where trust and loyalty were rare treasures. But within this close-knit group, in the heart of their struggle, a shocking betrayal loomed on the horizon, an unforeseen twist that would alter the course of their battle and force them to confront the ultimate test of their resolve.

With his scientific knowledge and passion for marine life, Dr Marcus had been a key figure in Tristan's group.

He had shared his vision of a protected and sustainable ocean and had initially fought with Tristan. Together, they had faced countless challenges and forged an unbreakable bond.

In the stillness of the ocean's depths, on a night filled with purpose, Tristan and Dr Marcus had taken on the solemn task of gathering critical data concerning the disheartening issue of underwater water pollution. Amid their vital work, Dr Marcus's communication device lit up with an incoming transmission, its source veiled in encryption. Dr Marcus's furrowed brow revealed the gravity of the message he had just received, a secret he chose to guard for the time being, withholding its contents from Tristan and the rest of the group. The encrypted missive hung in the water, a mystery that would soon unfold and alter the course of their mission.

As time passed, Tristan noticed that Dr Marcus became more and more distant and reserved. He had lost his enthusiasm for the cause and seemed distracted by his secret shelter responsibilities. Tristan began to worry about the strange attitude of his friend and ally.

After nights of keeping the encrypted secret close to his chest, the tension reached its breaking point one evening. His eyes heavy with the weight of the concealed message, Dr Marcus finally summoned Tristan and the rest of their group. With a deep breath, he confessed the reason behind his secretive behaviour. He had been engaged in covert correspondence with an enigmatic figure who professed to hold a treasure trove of invaluable information about the corporate machinations. Dr Marcus had clandestinely forged an alliance with this contact, their shared objectives converging with the hope of bolstering their struggle with irrefutable proof and exposing the truth to the world.

The revelation hung in the water, which could prove to be their greatest asset or their most profound test.

Distrust hung heavily in the confined underwater space as Tristan and the others processed Dr Marcus's revelation. The secrecy surrounding this newfound collaboration had stirred a simmering pot of scepticism and apprehension. They questioned why Dr Marcus had concealed his involvement, suspecting potential hidden agendas and uncertainty. Nevertheless, the urgency of their cause led them to a reluctant consensus: they would at least entertain the contact's revelations and determine whether it could truly be a game-changing asset in their fight for justice and truth. The high-stakes waters of betrayal and trust were becoming increasingly treacherous. The meeting with the contact took place in an isolated underwater cave, far from his secret shelter. Tristan, Dr Marcus, and Black Neptune encountered the mysterious individual, partially hidden in the shadows.

The contact's voice resonated through the dimly lit space, his words a revelation amid the tension-filled air. He unveiled astonishing information about the corporations and their hidden mastermind. His assertive words painted a vivid picture: he possessed the concrete evidence required to expose the corporations' illegal dealings, evidence that would likely lead to their legal downfall.

Even more intriguing was his claim to possess access to advanced technology, a digital arsenal

with the potential to dismantle corporate secrets further and lay their intricate web of corruption bare. A potentially game-changing ally seemed to have entered the fold in this underground struggle for justice.

During the contact's narrative, an uneasy atmosphere permeated the room. Tristan, Dr Marcus, and the rest of the group exchanged wary glances. Something about the unfolding situation struck them as off-kilter. It was as if this enigmatic informant held a strangely deep knowledge of their struggle, almost too conveniently so.

This raised suspicions about the true motives behind this contact's sudden appearance, making the group question whether they could trust the presented

information entirely. This underwater realm of intrigue and uncertainty blurred the line between ally and adversary.

Finally, Tristan made a bold decision. He asked the contact to reveal his true identity and the motivations behind his collaboration. The individual hesitated momentarily and then revealed his face with a quick gesture.

Surprise and shock reverberated throughout the cavern as the group's eyes widened with recognition. Their mysterious informant was none other than Donovan, the former Neptec security leader they believed to be vanquished in the depths of the submarine battle. His unexpected reappearance sent ripples of astonishment through the room. The realisation that Donovan had not perished but had plotted in the shadows since their last encounter left them all in disbelief and apprehension.

The dynamics of trust and betrayal were once again thrust into the spotlight.

The betrayal of a close friend and ally shook Tristan and his group. They could not believe Dr Marcus had secretly collaborated with Donovan, one of their most formidable enemies. Trust had been shattered, and unanswered questions filled the cave.

Donovan unravelled the story of his survival and the elaborate scheme he had hatched. He described how he had narrowly escaped their previous battle and had meticulously orchestrated his return to the underwater world. His agenda had been driven by a thirst for power and wealth, using his intimate knowledge of the corporations' inner workings. Donovan had expertly manipulated Dr Marcus, exploiting his desire for additional evidence in their struggle. He revealed his intention to leverage the information he had gathered for personal gain, disregarding the group's mission for justice and truth. The group, now painfully aware of the depth of Donovan's deception, grappled with the harsh realities of betrayal and mistrust.

Tristan, furious and betrayed, demanded that Donovan leave the cave immediately. Knowing that he had lost the trust of Tristan and his party, Donovan withdrew from the cave, leaving everyone in shock.

The group's trust in Dr Marcus had been unshaken, making his betrayal even more devastating. Tristan and the others had leaned on his wisdom and guidance throughout their struggle, and the revelation of his collaboration with Donovan hit them like a tidal wave. They were left grappling with an unexpected turn of events, plagued by a newfound sense of vulnerability. The presence of Donovan, a known adversary with insider knowledge of their operations, cast a shadow of uncertainty over their mission for justice and truth. It was a stark reminder of their complex and perilous underwater battle. The betrayal of a close friend had left a deep mark on Tristan and his group.

The betrayal of a close friend had left a deep mark on Tristan and his group.

They realised they must be even more cautious and determined in their struggle for justice and truth. They couldn't let Donovan's betrayal stop them from exposing powerful corporations and protecting the ocean. The fight was far from over, and they faced even greater challenges.

Chapter 17

THE RACE AGAINST TIME

The betrayal of Donovan, a former ally who had become a traitor, left Tristan and his group in shock and distrust. They had trusted Dr Marcus and had never expected that he would betray their cause in such a way. Now, they faced a new plot twist, with Donovan's threat and his insider knowledge of corporations.

Donovan's shocking betrayal underscored the pressing necessity for comprehensive knowledge about the inner workings of the corporations and the advanced marine technology they held.

Tristan and his comrades understood that the consequences of Donovan's actions could be catastrophic, jeopardising their mission and the entire underwater world. They recognised the

urgency of regaining control over the situation, preventing Donovan from exploiting the information he possessed, and once again shifting the balance of power in their favour. The race for truth and justice in the ocean's depths had taken yet another unexpected twist.

Time became a critical resource in their struggle. The Neptec and Aquadyne corporations continued to pursue them relentlessly, and Donovan had valuable information that could further expose the corporations.

The race to get that information and use it to protect the ocean became more pressing than ever.

Tristan and his determined companions convened in the dimly lit underwater cave for an intense discussion. They were acutely aware that they stood at a critical juncture. To counter Donovan's betrayal and prevent the potential disaster he posed, they had to strategise and execute their next moves meticulously. Their primary objectives were to halt Donovan's nefarious plans, regain control of the crucial information he held, and secure more irrefutable evidence of the corporation's illicit actions. Their quest for justice and truth had entered a pivotal phase where their every decision could alter the course of their struggle.

In the clandestine realm of the underwater digital network, Black Neptune intensified his efforts. He delved into the depths of the cyber world, tirelessly scouring for breadcrumbs that would unveil Donovan's whereabouts and provide essential leads. The stakes were higher than ever. The advanced marine technology in Donovan's clutches was a potent tool that could be wielded to their advantage, and Tristan was unwavering in his resolve to prevent its misuse.

This digital hunt was a race against time, a quest to outsmart Donovan and secure the critical technology. Their struggle had taken on a new layer of complexity, where every line of code and encrypted message could sway the balance of power.

His face marked with a profound sense of guilt; Dr Marcus humbly accepted his responsibility for Donovan's treachery. He spoke sincerely and vowed to be crucial in their quest to unearth the truth.

Standing before Tristan and the rest of the group, he openly admitted to his grave mistake in trusting Donovan. Determination glimmered in his eyes as he declared his unwavering commitment to mending the damage he had unwittingly caused. In the face of his blunder, he was determined to right the wrongs and prove his allegiance to the cause.

As they progressed in their search for information about Donovan and the corporations, Tristan and his group realised they needed to find allies in underwater society who shared their cause. They needed to form a coalition of individuals and groups committed to ocean protection and justice.

One fateful night, while venturing into the ocean's hidden depths, Tristan and Black Neptune stumbled upon a group of underwater scientists diligently researching the enigmatic marine technology possessed by the corporations. Their chance encounter ignited a spark of hope within the group, as these scientists willingly opened their troves of knowledge and insights about the advanced technology.

They divulged their remarkable findings, providing crucial information that could potentially neutralise the corporations' technological advantage.

The information shared by the underwater scientists was nothing short of a revelation for Tristan and his dedicated team. It offered hope and a tangible path toward neutralising the formidable threat of advanced corporate marine technology. The newly recruited scientists became invaluable allies, throwing their collective knowledge and expertise behind Tristan's mission. Together, they forged a comprehensive plan to disable the technology that had

empowered the corporations for so long, levelling the playing field in their fight for justice and truth.

The passage of time seemed to speed up as Tristan and his steadfast allies pushed forward with their mission. With every moment that passed, the sense of urgency intensified. They were acutely aware that the corporations would not relent in their relentless pursuit of Donovan, and they were more than willing to deploy their formidable advanced marine technology to safeguard their interests.

The endeavour to secure this technology and successfully deactivate it quickly became the linchpin of their entire cause. The future of the underwater world hinged on this high-stakes battle of wits and determination.

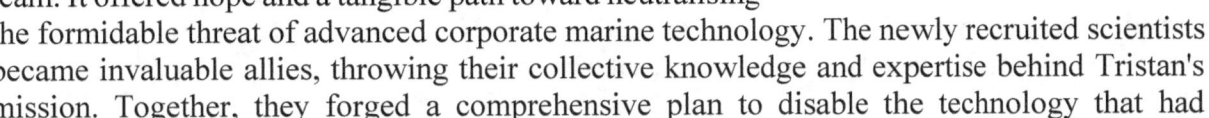

Tristan recognised that in addition to thwarting Donovan's treacherous plans and neutralising corporate marine technology, it was imperative to find a means of completely unveiling the corporations' illicit activities. Getting this critical information into the hands of both the authorities and the wider public was essential to ensuring that the truth would come to light and that justice would be served. The task of gathering concrete evidence and orchestrating a strategic, hard-hitting exposé had now become a central component of their multifaceted mission.

He had to ensure that the truth arose and that corporations were held accountable for their actions.

Under Black Neptune's guidance and the underwater scientists' expertise, Tristan and his allies form ulated a daring strategy to infiltrate one of the corporations' marine energy extraction facilities.

This plan was nothing short of audacious, recognising the challenges and staunch opposition they would encounter within the facility's fortified walls. Their unwavering commitment to the cause and the safeguarding of the ocean spurred them to make this high-stakes gamble, fully aware that they were placing everything on the line for the pursuit of justice and the greater good.

As the night of the mission drew nearer, Tristan and his group meticulously readied themselves, ensuring they had all the equipment and resources necessary for the upcoming infiltration. They were acutely aware that they were locked in a race against time, with every second holding immense significance. The intensification of the battle over advanced marine technology had left them with the unmistakable feeling that the sands of time were slipping away.

The urgency to secure and utilise that critical information to safeguard the oceans had never been more palpable. It was a pivotal moment in their struggle, demanding their determination and resilience.

As they made their final preparations for the upcoming daring mission, Tristan and his devoted group remained steadfast in their resolve. Their determination was unwavering, and they steeled themselves to confront any challenge or hurdle that came their way. In their unwavering pursuit of justice and safeguarding the ocean, they were ready to face whatever adversities lay ahead, knowing that the stakes were higher than ever.

Chapter 18

THE FINAL CONFRONTATION

The infiltration mission at one of the corporations' marine energy extraction facilities was underway. Tristan and his group had meticulously prepared every detail, aware that they were in a race against time to get the information they needed to protect the ocean and expose the illegal activities of corporations.

The marine energy extraction facility they had their sights on was nothing short of an underwater fortress, shrouded in secrecy and heavily fortified. It was safeguarded by a formidable corps of armed guards and a sophisticated web of advanced security systems. The knowledge that they would encounter robust opposition did little to sway their determination. Their unwavering commitment to the cause and the ocean's safeguard compelled them to stake everything on this perilous mission, fully aware of the monumental challenges ahead.

In the daring raid, Tristan assumed the role of the group's leader, with Dr Marcus, Black Neptune, and the dedicated underwater scientists forming the vanguard.

They ventured into the ocean's depths with a shared purpose and unwavering resolve, navigating the underwater world with stealth and precision.

Their journey was characterised by a deep understanding of the intricate underwater currents and a mastery of their specialised equipment, allowing them to evade corporate security systems' watchful eye. The collaborative efforts of this diverse team made them a formidable force against the corporate fortress they aimed to breach.

As they approached the facility, the tension in the group increased. They knew they were about to face the final confrontation with corporate leaders and that the success of their mission could change the course of the struggle.

Upon reaching their destination, the marine energy extraction facility loomed, an imposing underwater structure with powerful floodlights illuminating the surrounding water. They could see armed guards vigilantly patrolling the premises, their presence a formidable obstacle.

Corporate security systems were on high alert, creating an aura of tension and danger that only intensified the group's determination to

expose the corporations' illegal activities and protect the ocean. The scene was fraught with the anticipation of a high-stakes confrontation, where every move would be crucial to the success of their mission.

Tristan and his intrepid group plunged even deeper, employing the cover of shadows and exploiting underwater currents to evade detection. Black Neptune, their tech-savvy ally, worked diligently to infiltrate the complex security systems, diverting the guards' attention and systematically disabling surveillance cameras to create a safe path for their infiltration.

The mission was fraught with tension and peril as the team encountered a series of unforeseen challenges. Every step they took was met with uncertainty, from bypassing formidable security measures to navigating uncharted waters and unpredictable underwater currents. Their resolve and resilience were tested, but their commitment to exposing corporate wrongdoing and safeguarding the ocean bolstered their determination to overcome each obstacle.

Tristan and the others were determined to get to the main control room, hoping to find the needed information.

At long last, they reached the heart of the facility, the central control room, where high-ranking corporate executives were orchestrating the operations of marine energy extraction. To their astonishment, the very leaders of Neptec and Aquadyne were in attendance, fully aware of the audacious threat Tristan and his resolute group posed.

The stage was set for the ultimate showdown. With courage and determination, Tristan confronted the corporate leaders, demanding accountability for their illicit actions and explaining their malevolent intent regarding advanced marine technology.

The corporate leaders, fearing the unravelling of their ill-gotten empire, did not hesitate to respond aggressively, plunging them into

a perilous confrontation that would determine the fate of the ocean and its guardians.

An underwater battle of epic proportions erupted within the confines of the control room. Tristan and his determined group found themselves pitted against a formidable ensemble of heavily armed corporate guards and the ruthless leaders of Neptec and Aquadyne. It was a perilous clash, with the stakes higher than ever, as the outcome hung in the balance.

The battle unfolded with unrelenting intensity and constant danger. Submarine energy weapons discharged in all directions, creating chaotic explosions and powerful shockwaves reverberating throughout the aquatic realm. A serene underwater

environment was now transformed into a tumultuous battlefield. Tristan and the corporate leaders locked eyes in a deadly face-off, their battle echoing with the urgency of their mission to secure vital information and advanced marine technology.

During the ongoing battle, Tristan's acute understanding of the underwater world and its inhabitants became his trump card. Recognising that he needed every advantage to secure the upper hand, he harnessed his unique ability to communicate with the diverse denizens of the ocean.

With intricate gestures and vocalisations, he summoned a formidable alliance of marine creatures, including a pod of highly intelligent dolphins and a school of sleek, powerful sharks. These majestic sea creatures swiftly joined the fray, rallying behind Tristan to tip the scales in their favour.

The arrival of the allied marine creatures marked a profound turning point in the battle. With their innate prowess, the dolphins exhibited unparalleled agility and intelligence, executing coordinated manoeuvres that bewildered and disoriented the corporate guards.

Meanwhile, the sharks brought an imposing presence, striking terror into the hearts of the corporate leaders. Their combined efforts reshaped the battlefield dynamics entirely, bestowing Tristan's group a revitalised sense of determination and impetus.

The control room transformed into tumultuous and pandemonium as the conflict escalated. It became a theatre of chaos as the intense submarine battle reached its dramatic climax.

Underwater energy weapons sparked and sputtered, resulting in spectacular displays of illuminated explosions reverberating underwater with shockwaves. Amidst the fervent struggle, Tristan and his comrades tenaciously pressed forward, empowered by the unwavering support of their newfound allies from the depths.

In a climactic showdown, Tristan found himself face-to-face with the conspiracy's mastermind,

the orchestrator behind Neptec's sinister agenda. Tristan triumphed over his adversary after a gruelling and fierce combat marked by a whirlwind of martial prowess. He skilfully disarmed the corporate leader, shattering the illusion of invulnerability that had cloaked him.

With the corporate leaders vanquished, the marine energy extraction facility lay under Tristan's control. This pivotal moment allowed Tristan and his dedicated group to gain unfettered access to the vital information they had long sought. As they sifted through the digital records and classified documents, they unveiled incontrovertible proof of the corporations' nefarious activities. They also unearthed the coveted details surrounding the advanced marine technology that had spurred their relentless pursuit of justice.

The victory in the final confrontation was bittersweet. Tristan and his group had faced countless challenges and sacrificed much in their fight for justice and the protection of the ocean. Now, they had the information and technology they needed, but they knew their fight wasn't over.

Exposing the illegal activities of corporations and disabling advanced marine technology were important steps in the right direction, but corporations remained powerful and dangerous.

 Tristan knew he had to bring the truth to the authorities and the public so that corporations would be held accountable for their actions.

The final confrontation in the depths of the ocean had been an epic battle, but the fight for justice and protection of the ocean was far from over. Tristan and his group prepared to face the next chapter of their struggle, determined to press forward with courage and determination.

Chapter **19**

THE FALL OF CORPORATIONS

After a long struggle for justice and the protection of the ocean, the time finally came when the corporations that had exerted inordinate control over the seas and advanced marine technology were on the verge of defeat. Tristan's courageous choice to reveal the truth and promote the responsible use of technology resulted in a monumental shift in humanity's relationship with the ocean.

The inception of the international governing body entrusted with the oversight of advanced marine technology marked a pivotal turning point in the world's commitment to safeguarding the ocean's integrity. Imposing stringent regulations on its utilisation, this body had been established to guarantee that the technology was harnessed judiciously, sustainably, and for the collective good. This monumental transformation signified a profound reorientation of priorities, with the paramount focus on preserving the ocean and its diverse life forms.

Formerly seen as indomitable and dominant, corporations found themselves in a radically altered landscape. As they navigated the shifting tides, they encountered growing opposition and faced escalating scrutiny from the global community. The once-overpowering entities now had to grapple with mounting challenges to their authority and a pressing need to align their actions with the world's renewed commitment to ocean protection.

The unveiling of their illicit activities and ruthless exploitation of the ocean instigated a profound transformation in both public sentiment and corporate standing.

Corporate executives embarked on an ardent battle to safeguard their vested interests and preserve their diminishing influence. However, they found themselves ensnared by an incontrovertible body of evidence that left them with no credible counterarguments. The substantial and compelling proof of their unlawful activities and rapacious behaviour towards the ocean was irrefutable in the eyes of the courts and the public.

Government authorities, alongside influential international organisations, launched a sweeping crackdown on these corporations. This encompassed rigorous and comprehensive investigations that led to the filing of charges for a range of financial and environmental transgressions. Corporate leaders found themselves entangled in lengthy and intricate legal proceedings, during which the full scale of their misdeeds was brought to light. These trials served to underscore the severity and scale of their crimes, leading to monumental shifts in the perception of corporate accountability and the significance of protecting the environment.

During these trials, the entire world became transfixed by the flagrant illegalities committed by corporations and the urgency of safeguarding the ocean.

Civil society, stirred by a shared commitment to environmental preservation, coalesced to form a formidable alliance that sought accountability and justice. Environmental activists, marine conservation proponents, and impassioned individuals who cared deeply about the planet's well-being came together, raising their voices and organising for change.

Their collective efforts sent ripples of fervour across the globe as they called for corporations to answer for their ecological and ethical transgressions.

Under this unrelenting and protracted wave of public outcry, magnified by the ceaseless scrutiny of the media, the once-impervious corporations confronted an abrupt reversal of their fortunes. Their staunch supporters dwindled in number, and the once-indomitable influence they wielded began to erode, marking a seismic shift in the broader sociopolitical landscape. With the world's attention increasingly focused on accountability and environmental stewardship issues, corporations were compelled to confront the far-reaching repercussions of their actions and the transformative recalibration of the corporate realm.

The culmination of these developments arrived in the form of a final verdict handed down in the trials, and it proved to be nothing short of catastrophic for the corporations. Corporate leaders found themselves held accountable for a litany of financial and environmental infractions, facing not only substantial monetary fines but also sentences of imprisonment.

Furthermore, they were mandated to pay substantial reparations for the extensive harm inflicted upon the ocean and its myriad inhabitants, thereby making long-overdue amends for their previously unchecked transgressions.

The downfall of corporations served as an epochal turning point in the ongoing battle for ocean conservation and justice. It symbolised the culmination of an era dominated by avarice and authority, in which responsibility and sustainability had been eclipsed. The aftermath of this transformative period witnessed the gradual restoration and safeguarding of the ocean and the emergence of a new beginning.

Tristan and his intrepid group were hailed as heroes and the stalwart defenders of the ocean. Their unwavering valour and tenacity had not only altered the course of underwater history but had also charted a course toward a brighter, more promising future.

Their indomitable spirit bore witness to the notion that a resolute collective could challenge the supremacy of corporations, champion the cause of justice, and become ardent advocates for the protection and preservation of the ocean. Their legacy resonated with all those whom their tireless dedication had touched.

As the corporate giants crumbled, comprehensive measures were swiftly implemented to rejuvenate and safeguard the oceanic realm. Large-scale clean-up initiatives were undertaken, enlisting the efforts of dedicated volunteers to rid the aquatic environment of pollution and to mend the ailing marine ecosystems. The establishment of extensive marine protected areas took shape, serving as sanctuaries where the astounding biodiversity could flourish and offering a refuge for species threatened by overexploitation.

A prevailing sense of serenity appeared on the horizon for the underwater world. A newfound unity permeated the underwater society, as individuals from all walks of life banded together to pursue a common cause — the defence and preservation of the ocean.

With an ethos of shared responsibility for its well-being, the collaborative application of advanced marine technology could be a transformative force that no longer pillaged the ocean but contributed to its sustainability.

The legacy of past struggles had set the stage for a harmonious coexistence between humanity and the ocean, fuelled by the spirit of reverence, stewardship, and collective dedication.

Tristan and his dedicated group remained steadfast as guardians of the ocean, actively participating in the ongoing initiatives to preserve its delicate ecosystems. Their involvement extended to vital marine conservation activities and diligent monitoring of ocean health, ensuring their commitment to protecting the ocean remained unwavering. The cause that once led them to confront formidable corporate forces continued to motivate their tireless efforts in safeguarding the underwater realm.

The resumption of peace and harmony within the underwater world was palpable. The ocean and its inhabitants now thrived in a revitalised and pristine environment. This renewal in oceanic health served as a testament to the efficacy of collective conservation endeavours and the enduring resilience of marine ecosystems.

A renewed sense of understanding had permeated the human psyche, emphasising the crucial role of environmental stewardship and the imperative of coexisting harmoniously with the ocean.

The transformation beneath the ocean's surface was not contained to its depths alone. The resounding success in the battle against corporate greed and the rebirth of the underwater world served as an inspirational example for the surface world. Humanity, awakened to the urgency of environmental conservation, shifted its focus toward protecting the oceans and preserving natural resources. The legacy of Tristan and his

group's unwavering commitment became a catalyst for a broader movement, fostering a deeper appreciation for the planet's interconnected ecosystems.

Tristan's legacy as a champion of justice and ocean protection transcended the underwater world and etched an enduring mark on human history. His tale underscored the capacity of a determined few to incite transformation and inspire a global consciousness geared towards preserving our world's most precious and vital resource — the ocean.

Their courage and determination had shown that, even in the face of daunting challenges, determined action could prevail and lead to change.

With peace and protection of the ocean assured, Tristan and his group looked to a future where humanity and the ocean lived in harmony. His courageous choice and commitment to justice made that future possible, and his legacy would live on for generations.

Chapter **20**

A NEW DAWN

Following the fall of the corporations and the triumphant struggle for ocean justice, the underwater world stood on the threshold of a new era. The battles had inflicted scars upon the ocean's depths but unlocked the potential for a future where the oceans and humanity coexisted harmoniously.

Reconstruction became the immediate priority. The ocean and the underwater cities bore the physical marks of the conflict, necessitating extensive repair and rehabilitation. Advanced marine technology was harnessed to expedite the clean-up and restoration efforts, ensuring a swift recovery. In this endeavour, sea creatures played a vital role, collaborating with their human counterparts to revive damaged ecosystems.

Underwater cities once again began to flourish, returning to their former vibrancy. The resurgent underwater communities embraced marine conservation as a core value. Rigorous regulations were implemented to safeguard the ocean and its diverse biodiversity.

Robust research initiatives delved into the intricate intricacies of marine ecosystems, enhancing our understanding and fortifying the pillars of long-term sustainability.

During this transformative era, Tristan and his steadfast companions ascended to unrivalled leadership in marine conservation. They embarked on a ceaseless mission to meticulously monitor the ocean's well-being and diligently enforce the regulations designed to protect it. Their unwavering commitment to safeguarding the ocean retained its unwavering brilliance, and their influence swelled as they garnered the admiration and respect of the underwater society. Through their untiring dedication, they acted as vital navigators, guiding the underwater world toward a more brilliant, enduring, and sustainable future.

As the ocean recovered, advanced marine technology began to take on a more prominent role in benefiting humanity. Innovative technological strides gave rise to clean and sustainable marine energy sources, progressively supplanting the reliance on fossil fuels.

The adoption of renewable energy sources by underwater cities and fleets of waterborne vehicles was a landmark shift with far-reaching implications. As they transitioned away from dependence on corporations, these underwater communities significantly enhanced their sustainability and eco-friendliness. This transition marked a momentous departure from the environmentally damaging practices of the past, ushering in a future characterised by harmony, respect for the environment, and sustainable coexistence.

Furthermore, advanced marine technology found a new and vital role in scientific research. Underwater scientists harnessed its full potential to delve into comprehensive studies of the ocean and its diverse inhabitants. This employment of technology yielded a treasure trove of knowledge, driving significant breakthroughs in marine conservation and a deeper understanding of the intricate web of underwater biodiversity.

Harmony and serenity had been re-established in the underwater world. Coastal cities and shallow societies began to adopt a more reverent and cautious approach to the ocean.

A heightened global awareness of the need to protect the oceans had taken root, prompting the implementation of robust measures aimed at curbing pollution and stemming the exploitation of marine resources. This marked a monumental transformation in how humanity interacted with the underwater world, epitomising the resilience of the human spirit and its capacity for positive change.

The collaborative spirit between the underwater and surface worlds deepened as both realms recognised the importance of unified efforts to tackle global challenges impacting the oceans, including climate change and pollution. The establishment of international partnerships exemplified a shared commitment to safeguarding the health and sustainability of the ocean, transcending barriers that had once divided these two societies.

The synergy between underwater and surface communities became a cornerstone in their shared endeavour to protect the ocean and its precious resources.

Tristan and his dedicated group continued to serve as tireless advocates and inspirational leaders in marine conservation.

Their unwavering dedication to preserving the ocean remained an unchanging source of inspiration for individuals worldwide. Their ongoing work ignited a collective passion in others to join the noble cause, reinforcing the belief that collective action was vital in securing a healthier and more sustainable future for the underwater world and beyond.

In harmonious collaboration, they toiled ceaselessly to secure a future where the ocean and humanity would flourish.

The underwater world was greeted by a new era, leaving behind the scars of war and corporate tyranny to embrace hope and the prospects of a brighter tomorrow.

The ocean, once wounded, was now in a state of rejuvenation and abundance, while humanity was learning the invaluable lesson of coexisting in perfect accord with it.

Sea creatures, long-suffering under the weight of human exploitation, were now the inhabitants of an environment that was not just cleaner but healthier, brimming with vitality.

Coral reefs displayed vibrant recoveries, fish populations multiplied, and the waters regained their pristine clarity, evoking awe and wonder.

The underwater society gazed ahead with unyielding hope and an unshakable resolve. Having surmounted monumental challenges, they proved that resolute action could indeed triumph over the grasp of avarice and tyranny. Their commitment to protecting and living in harmony with the ocean was an enduring legacy to be passed on to future generations, forging a path toward a world where humanity and the ocean thrived.

As the sun set on the underwater horizon, marking the end of a day filled with activity and hope, the underwater world prepared for a new dawn. A dawn in which the ocean and humanity would walk together towards a fut ure of peace, prosperity and sustainability.

Chapter **21**

EPILOGUE: TRISTAN'S LEGACY

Tristan's legacy proved to be enduring, transcending the dark chapters of war and corporate oppression. His unwavering courage and tireless commitment to safeguarding the ocean became a lighthouse of hope, an embodiment of resilience, and a template for the generations that would succeed him. His remarkable contribution to humanity's future, intertwined with the well-being of the world's oceans, became a celebrated story echoing across the globe.

Following their triumph against the corporations and the restoration of the ocean, Tristan and his steadfast group remained steadfast in their roles as ardent ocean advocates. They devoted themselves to monitoring the

ocean's health, championing marine conservation, and ensuring the resolute enforcement of regulations. Their commitment never faltered, and the sphere of their influence continued to expand as they earned the admiration and esteem of both the submerged and surface societies.

Tristan's prominence in the worldwide campaign for marine conservation became indelible. He received invitations to international conferences and prominent events to share his unparalleled wealth of experience and knowledge in ocean protection, his voice echoing as a clarion call for preserving the world's precious marine ecosystems.

The progress catalysed by advanced marine technology extended to the scientific realm, where underwater scientists harnessed its potential to gain unprecedented insights into the oceans and their captivating denizens. This technological boon yielded momentous advances in marine conservation and the quest for a more profound understanding of underwater biodiversity.

Tristan's legacy resonated not only in the annals of history but also in the collective consciousness of society. Both the submerged and surface communities began to view the ocean with newfound reverence and responsibility. Committed to safeguarding the marine environment, they implemented measures to curb pollution and the unsustainable exploitation of marine resources.

Environmental conservation emerged as a guiding light for future generations, signifying an enduring commitment to the ocean and its delicate ecosystems.

The unification of the submerged and surface worlds gained momentum as they fortressed their collaboration. International partnerships were forged, underscoring the necessity of transcending global challenges that affected the oceans, notably climate change and pollution. The synergy between the two domains evolved into a bedrock of foundational importance for ensuring the long-term well-being and sustainability of the ocean.

Tristan's legacy radiated outward, touching younger generations' hearts from the submerged and surface societies. His extraordinary tale of valour and unwavering commitment to safeguarding the ocean kindled a fire of inspiration among the youth, and they took up his mantle with resolve. Pledging to ensure a sustainable future for the ocean and humanity, they embraced his legacy as a guiding light.

Over time, Tristan's name evolved into a symbol of courage and dedication to ocean protection. Monumental tributes to his indomitable spirit sprang up in underwater cities across the globe, serving as enduring testaments to his profound impact. In educational institutions, Tristan's story became a cornerstone of inspiration, motivating countless generations to uphold the values of ocean conservation and the relentless pursuit of a harmonious coexistence with the sea.

Tristan's profound legacy extended well beyond the confines of the underwater world, resonating with both submerged and surface societies, leading humanity to recognise the paramount importance of cherishing the ocean and fostering harmonious coexistence. This newfound understanding catalysed the implementation of extensive, interconnected measures designed to combat pollution, nurture biodiversity, and champion safeguarding the world's oceans.

These initiatives inaugurated an era of collective responsibility for our planet's invaluable aquatic ecosystems.

What was once an ocean ravaged by corporate avarice and exploitation underwent a remarkable transformation, emerging as a poignant symbol of hope and recovery.

Coral reefs flourished once more, fish populations rebounded, and the waters themselves reclaimed their former crystalline purity, becoming pristine havens of beauty and wonder. Once taken for granted and pillaged, the ocean now stood as a testament to the positive changes brought about by humanity's united commitment to its protection and care.

Tristan's enduring legacy was etched into the collective memory of all touched by his inspiring journey. His story was a timeless reminder that courage and determination, when harnessed for a noble cause, could truly change the world. He kindled the flames of passion within future generations, instilling in them the fervour to rise in defence of the ocean and recognise the transformative power within their grasp.

As time marched on and successive generations inherited the fruits of Tristan and his group's labour, a profound harmony enveloped the ocean and humanity.

Tristan's legacy transcended the confines of his era and continued to illuminate the path ahead, serving as a guiding star in the night sky of hope. His legacy acted as a beacon, reminding humanity that, when united, they held the power to shield the ocean and secure a sustainable future for all. Thus, as the underwater sun dipped below the horizon, signifying the culmination of an era marked by struggle and transformation, Tristan's legacy shimmered brightly like a star, gently leading humanity toward a future where the ocean and society coexisted in perfect harmony.

www.ingramcontent.com/pod-product-compliance
Lightning Source LLC
Chambersburg PA
CBHW080851120626

46546CB00008B/2787